I WAS HOPING TO AGE LIKE FINE WINE BUT I'M FEELING MORE LIKE AN AVOCADO

by

Marlene Kern Fischer

TELEMACHUS PRESS

I Was Hoping To Age Like A Fine Wine But I'm Feeling More Like An Avocado

COVER AND INTERIOR ART AND DESIGN BY DANIELLE CLEMONS

Photographs used with permission

Jewish Space Laser Corps patch - Weitzman National Museum of Jewish History - www.shoptheweitzman.org

Publishing Services by Telemachus Press, LLC
7652 Sawmill Road, Suite 304
Dublin, Ohio 43016
http://www.telemachuspress.com

ISBN: 978-1-956867-96-1 (eBook)
ISBN: 978-1-956867-95-4 (paperback)

HUMOR / Family and Relationships

Version 2024.05.09

For Turkey Baby

INTRODUCTION

Ten years ago if you had told me that I was going to write three books and have a blog on Facebook with 57K followers, I wouldn't have believed you. In fact, I probably would have been a little concerned about your well-being.

But here I am—60 years old with this amazing third act that follows my first, very brief career in public relations and my second, much longer career raising my sons. I'm proof that there is still time for whatever it is you'd like to do.

This book wouldn't have been possible without a lot of people. Starting with my mates in Aisle 4 who make me think, laugh, share my words, and show me that there is still a lot of good in the world. Thank you for supporting me.

Thank you to my family who remain a constant source of material and who allow me to write about them. Especially my husband, who I sometimes lovingly refer to as Mr. Aisle 4. You always manage to find a typo in my work no matter how many times I've proofread it.

Thank you to my daughter-in-law Danielle, who has designed all my book covers. I love all our collaborations, workwise and other.

Thank you to my editor and friend Diane Schwemm, who believed in me all those years ago when I was still struggling to find my voice. You continue to make my words better.

Thank you to my rescue pup Maisy, who keeps me company when I write. Despite your barking, you're the best girl in the world.

Thank you to my publisher Steve Himes for your patience. You make publishing a book almost fun.

Thank you to the bookstores and local retailers who stock my books—especially Tazza Café, Sammy's Kosher Market, Scattered Books, Pleasantville Bookstore, and The Hickory Stick Bookstore.

Thank you to David Monasebian. I appreciate your enthusiasm and support.

I hope you all enjoy reading my stories, many of which originally appeared on my blog, *Thoughts From Aisle 4*, as much as I enjoyed writing them.

xo Marlene

FOREWORD

Marlene and I go way back to the days when I was a new editor and she was just getting started with *Thoughts From Aisle 4*. What a joy to work with her again and help edit her third book!

Why do we all love spending time with Marlene on her blog and in her books? I think it's because reading Marlene is like sharing a (hygge) mug of hot chocolate with an old friend—the one you don't have to dress up for, who's always there when you need her and loves you for exactly who you are.

First of all, of course, Marlene is funny, but her humor is appealing because it springs from a warm, generous heart. No one delivers a zinger quite like Marlene, but she also doesn't shy away from the stories that are harder to tell, the ones that hurt. Her voice is compassionate and honest. She is really and truly herself on every page. And I always feel as if I'm right there with her, sorting through boxes at her new house, pondering the mystery of having bought two identical pairs of shoes, or cradling her first grandchild in her arms.

Congratulations on your newest book, Marlene! I can't wait to turn the page and find out what happens next.

—Diane Schwemm

TABLE OF CONTENTS

3. FAMILY & FRIENDS: THE RELATIONSHIPS THAT GROUND ME

I WAS HOPING TO AGE
LIKE FINE WINE
BUT I'M FEELING MORE
LIKE AN AVOCADO

Being a boy mom means
your kid could be married
with nine kids and you
have no idea because he
never mentioned it

~Thoughts From Aisle 4

PART 1: PARENTING: I'M STILL AT IT

CIA BOY

*M*y youngest son phoned me from college today. We started chatting about his upcoming Birthright trip to Israel—he's going with eleven of his camp friends at the end of December.

He mentioned that they might extend their stay by a few days, so I told him that if they did, he would overlap with his middle brother and almost sister-in-law. They too are going on Birthright on January 1st.

"J and N are going on Birthright????? I didn't know that!! How didn't you tell me??"

As many of you know, I sometimes refer to this particular son as CIA Boy. I call him that because he hasn't told me much since he was recruited for the CIA when he was in middle school—possibly even before. Of course, I have no empirical proof of this since he hides his pay stubs or has direct deposit to a hidden bank account. Let's just say I came up with this theory because it would explain a whole lot.

Anyway, although he doesn't like sharing much information (or isn't allowed), he apparently gets deeply offended if someone neglects to give HIM information.

As we were talking about Israel, I told him that while he was there, if he happened to see a young man who looked like someone from our neighborhood, it was probably him, since he too is going on Birthright.

Now my son was completely outraged.

"What else haven't you told me?!?!"

Fortunately, I HAD divulged that we will be moving to a new house in the middle of December. Although it would have served him right if he came home for winter break and found other people living here and his room turned into a den.

Shoe on the other foot, people.

With three sons, I honestly sometimes forget who I told what to. In addition, they have their own texting group called "Three Brothers and a Van," but I'm guessing not a lot has been going on in their chat, since currently no one seems to know anything about anyone.

I sometimes imagine that if I had three daughters they would be sharing more with one another, but I can't say for sure. I have a lot of daughter theories, many of which probably are way off base. They are just fantasies that roll around in my brain.

In any event, right before we hung up, I mysteriously said, "Who knows what else I haven't told you?" I figured it was probably a good way to get him to call me again soon.

MY FANTASY DAUGHTERS VS. MY ACTUAL SONS

The other night I was eating dinner outside at a restaurant when I saw a mom and her three children waiting for a table. There was a younger boy, who was busy playing on his phone and two older girls, maybe eleven and fourteen. (I'm going somewhere with this story, I promise.)

The girls were wearing matching white sundresses. They left for a few minutes and as they walked away, they held hands.

These were my fantasy children.

As you know, I have three sons. And growing up, they didn't wear matching anything unless they were going to a sporting event where they donned team jerseys. I tried putting them in matching clothes ONCE (okay, maybe twice) and they still threaten to report me to Child Protective Services (CPS) for doing it.

And although they are pretty close now, growing up they did not walk around holding hands. In fact, there were times they tried to kill each other. Let me tell you about Mother's Day circa a lot of years ago (my coffee hasn't kicked in yet, so I can't give you an actual date).

We were at a restaurant and the service was admittedly slow. (This was in the days before kids had electronic devices to keep them occupied.) So to amuse himself, my oldest son took his spoon and put it over the votive candle flame. And then he put the spoon on my middle son's hand to make him scream. Which he obligingly did. Loudly.

At the next table were two little girls in matching dresses. (Again with the matching clothes.) And they were sitting at their table quietly coloring.

I feel like I was a fairly good disciplinarian. I made sure there were consequences to bad behavior. But sometimes I was just too weary. After the spoon incident, it's possible I just rolled my eyes and offered them each a roll.

Maybe I thought that if I dressed my boys in matching clothes they would behave. And I think I was onto something because when they wore those matching team jerseys they didn't fight (they left that to the players on the field).

Yes, yes, I realize that girls fight. Of course they do. All siblings fight. It's part of the siblings contract. "By signing below we hereby acknowledge that we will try and make our mother crazy by fighting over the most ridiculous things possible."

But when I see girls in matching dresses, I remember my fantasy of angelic children who behave nicely in restaurants and hold hands when they walk down the street.

A RARE COMPLIMENT FROM MY SON

I was talking to my youngest son and his girlfriend, and she told me that my son had paid me a nice compliment.

I was like, "Wait, what? A compliment from my son?? Tell me more!"

As a little background: My son and his girlfriend attend a university in Waltham, Massachusetts. Two days a week they assistant teach at a local synagogue's Hebrew school. I think they do it because they enjoy it and to earn a little extra money.

On Sunday, they attended the Hebrew's school's mock seder—Passover is coming up and the kids were learning about the holiday.

Apparently, my son said to his girlfriend something to the effect of, "This is so boring, I can't believe my mom used to come to all these things."

There's a lot to unpack in that sentence. First, there's the fact that he noticed that back in the day I was there. I was ALWAYS there. For mock seders at our synagogue but also so much more. For all three of my sons for everything (except maybe some sports games). I always wondered if my kids really cared if I came to their activities, but I preferred to err on the side of showing up rather than having them blame me for being absent at some point into the future.

After I heard about this astounding comment from my son, I spoke to him on the phone and he asked me if I was bored when I went to his various things. The short answer: sometimes. In my opinion, a fair amount of the stuff schools asked parents to show up for was silly. I always said it was a good thing that I wasn't a brain surgeon taking time out from saving lives to watch the Halloween parade when after school I'd be seeing my child in his costume when I took him trick or treating.

(It's not like seeing him as a superhero at school was a surprise—we'd probably spent two hours at the store choosing the costume.) But, of course, I went.

And I went to all the field days and plays and concerts. I actually enjoyed the concerts, especially when my boys joined jazz band in high school. I miss those.

I went to famous person day when my kids dressed up as someone they had researched, and DARE (Drug Abuse Resistance Education). I already knew how to say "no," so I'm honestly not sure why I needed to be there. I was there for the Lunar New Year parade. I also went on a fair number of field trips, even though bus rides made me nauseated. My oldest son always wanted to sit next to me which at least made the ride a lot more pleasant.

Although I didn't enjoy every event, I did always enjoy seeing my children. I hoped they were happy to see me. I do remember them scanning the audience until they spotted me. And then we would both smile and wave. That same smile and wave every child and parent has done since the dawn of time.

When you're parenting, you don't always know what you're doing right or wrong. Sometimes judgment doesn't come for decades.

But it is nice when you get positive feedback. As Tevye in *Fiddler on the Roof* said, "It doesn't change a thing. But even so. After twenty-five years (or twenty or thirty) —It's nice to know."

RAISING CHILDREN IS EASY SAID NO ONE EVER

Every now and then I look at pictures of my boys when they were little. Gosh, were they cute. And I think to myself, "Why in the world did I ever think raising kids was so difficult? Look at how cherubic their faces are."

But then, I think a little harder and it starts coming back to me.

For instance, the middle one, with his sweet bowl haircut and dimples, well, he was a handful. Actually, they all were, but in different ways.

As a toddler, that middle one couldn't be left alone. Because invariably he'd get into some sort of trouble.

There was the time I planned on taking my two sons (third boy hadn't yet arrived on the scene) into the city for some activity. I don't recall what. My older son had the day off from school—the boys were around two and seven. I left the younger one in front of the TV, or maybe I told the older one to watch his younger brother, because I needed a few minutes to get dressed.

So there I was, in my bedroom throwing on some clothes, when my toddler appeared before me covered in what I thought was blood. Panic stricken, I examined him a little closer to discover he had tomato sauce all over him. (By the way, those few seconds I thought he had blood on him took about two years off my life. If I actually added up all the heart-stopping moments my boys provided, I'd probably be astonished that I'm still even alive.)

Apparently, my husband, who had gotten home from work around midnight the night before, had made himself a pizza bagel and then left the tomato sauce on the counter. Where my son found it. And then for some unknown reason proceeded to pour it on himself and the carpeted steps leading to the second floor. For good measure, he went into my older son's room and emptied the last of it onto his brother's beige rug before coming to find me.

I had no idea how to remove tomato sauce stains from the carpet, so I called a cleaning service which advised me to run, not walk, to the nearest grocery store and pick up white vinegar and club soda. I piled the kids into the car, purchased the necessary ingredients, and spent hours scrubbing the carpets. Needless to say, we did not make it into the city that day. But my husband did come home from work early and took the kids out to dinner so I could have a few minutes to myself and contemplate my life.

It was days like that one (and believe me when I say this was not an isolated incident) that drove me to the brink of insanity. Possibly over the brink.

It's easy to look at old photos and forget the hard times. Because those faces—my goodness, they really were adorable.

OUCH: WHEN PARENTING HURTS

In addition to the times my kids did things that were unintentionally mischievous or destructive, there were the times they were quite intentional in their actions.

I feel like someone out there might need to hear this today. If your child is being difficult or less than nice to you, don't take it personally. Which I know is easier said than done.

It's one of the hardest things about parenting. That child of yours, who you'd throw yourself in front of a moving train to save, says or does something that's quite frankly, mean.

Ouch.

It hurts. I know because I've been there many times. Actually I'm there right now with one of my sons.

But here's the thing. They don't really mean it. Perhaps they do in the moment, but not in the overall picture. They know you love them, and they love you back.

I hate that part of parenting. But sadly, it goes with the territory. (Along with worrying and keeping the fridge stocked when they are home.) You are the designated safe person upon whom your child can unload their frustrations with the world. In a weird way, it's a compliment.

There were times I knew I would never forgive my child because they pierced my heart so deeply. But of course I did because how could I not?

If you are the person who needed to hear this today, please know that you are not alone. It's just that not everyone talks about it.

As your child matures, the hurts will (hopefully) come less frequently. Until then, hang in there, mama.

**No one is happier than
a mom whose grown
kid has called to say hi.
Nothing else. Just hi.**

~Thoughts From Aisle 4

SEARCHING FOR PROOF OF LIFE

When I was seven or eight months pregnant with my oldest son, there was a period of several hours when I didn't feel him move.

Panicked, I called my husband at work. He happens to be one of the best guys in the world but what he said to me was one of the top ten dumbest things he's uttered in the 42 years I've known him. He said the following:

"Try not to think about it."

Um, sure? There's a very real possibility that I'm walking around with a dead baby inside me, but I won't think about it. Maybe I could read a book instead, tell myself a few jokes, or even go buy myself a new handbag. My anxiety was undoubtedly heightened by the fact that my first son died when he was ten days old.

So I tried a trick that I knew. (I figured if it didn't work, I would head over to my doctor.) I took a can of orange juice concentrate from the freezer and placed it on my belly. After a few moments, my baby rolled away from the cold. Phew. I guess he was just taking a nap and didn't like being disturbed. Not much has changed there.

Anyway, fast forward eighteen years and he's in college. And I barely hear from him even though he has a shiny new Blackberry (remember those??). So every once in a while, I do the equivalent of the frozen orange juice trick: I poke him on Facebook. That used to be a thing—you could poke someone, and they could poke you back.

Poking was perfect for kids away at school because they didn't have to say anything. It was basically just proof of life. Not too different from when my son did a little roll in my belly. I'm guessing the whole poking idea was invented by a mom who hadn't heard from her child in a while. Honestly, I wish Facebook would bring it back.

My son is now 32. And he has two younger brothers. My current version of frozen orange juice and poking looks more like texts, funny memes, and articles I send them. A thumbs up or an emoji is enough response for me.

I'm guessing cave parents drew on the walls and waited for their kids to respond when they were done hunting for food. That's what all those ancient markings are.

The need to connect to one's child is as old as time itself. Only the means have changed.

Because when we know they are fine, we are fine too.

**Moms never retire—
we go from active
duty to reserve**

~Thoughts From Aisle 4

A VIRAL BLOG POST THAT WASN'T MINE

Eight or nine years ago, my oldest son wrote a blog post in which he detailed four things grown sons want their moms to know.

Number one on his list was "No, we didn't read the article that you sent us." He even used a Venn diagram to illustrate his point, which was that basically they either read the article about their favorite band already, or they aren't going to read the ten articles about whatever health/safety issue we're concerned about because "they aren't as nervous as we are."

That blog post went viral. But since then, a few things have happened. First, my son, who is now 32, has gotten more nervous about things. In fact, he was the one to warn ME of the impending pandemic. And when I went out to the grocery store when Covid first hit, he freaked out. It's kind of gratifying to see our kids turn into us.

Second, although I do think about his blog post when I send him or one of his siblings an article, it hasn't stopped me. Like not even a little bit. Because sending articles is what moms do. My mom does it to me. In fact just this morning, she sent me an article about how there's going to be a civil war in the United States. What am I supposed to do with this information? Purchase a bayonet?

We send articles because we want our kids to know we are thinking about them. Which is all the time. We don't really think they are going to read every word. Sometimes just the headline is enough: "Ice Storm Expected for New England" or "Celebrity Groundhog Dies Shortly Before His Big Day." I sent them that second article because I wanted them to know that it wasn't Punxsutawney Phil who went to his heavenly burrow, just a second-rate groundhog named Mel. I also just wanted to say, "Hi, hope you are having a good day and I miss you." Which is probably why my mom sent me the civil war article. At least I hope that's why.

I'm grateful that the internet was invented because it's made nagging a lot easier for moms. In the old days, we had to clip articles and send them in the mail to be ignored. So much money saved on postage. I'm now going to scour the news to see what article my kids will have zero interest in reading.

A mom's work is never done.

When you're a boy mom
and you're with a girl mom
and she gets 14 texts and
2 calls about one outfit
and you can't remember if
you've spoken to your son
in the last week

~Thoughts From Aisle 4

A MOM'S GOTTA DO WHAT A MOM'S GOTTA DO

It was his own fault really.

I'm talking about my youngest son, aka CIA Boy. In keeping with his secret profession, he keeps things close to the vest. Really close.

At one point earlier in his college years, though we hadn't heard anything about him dating, I suspected that my son had a girlfriend. Let's just say it was a mother's intuition. But I didn't know for sure until one of his brothers accidentally let it slip that the youngest was seeing someone.

As I mentioned before, my three boys are generally pretty good at guarding each other's secrets. I'm glad they are close and don't mind the don't-tell-mom aspect of their relationship.

So of course, after my hunch about the girlfriend, whose name I learned through her mom, who followed my blog and knew our kids were dating but wasn't allowed to let on, was confirmed, my husband and I took to stalking her on social media. I advised my husband to leave this delicate work to me because stalking is best left to the professionals and he's a novice.

You can guess what happened next. Yup, he violated the first rule of stalking and accidentally friend-requested the young woman. Yikes.

When my son found out, he yelled at his brothers via text for breaking the brothers' code of secrecy. Which both denied but told me about. For the record, they are all really good at denying things. "It wasn't me" was their battle cry for decades.

Desperate to undo the damage, my husband, who was mortified, went on Facebook and posted that he had been hacked and any recent friend requests should be disregarded as they had not come from him. I have no idea if my son bought it or not, but we all let the matter drop.

A few weeks later, CIA Boy mentioned his girlfriend because he wanted to bring her home. When I acted surprised to hear he was seeing someone, he said he had told me about her weeks ago. The old "let's try and make mom think she's crazy" trick. I'm onto their attempts at gaslighting me.

The couple ended up not being able to leave campus because of a new Covid outbreak and subsequent no-travel policy enacted by their university. So we zoomed our Passover seder during which we met the girlfriend virtually. Who is truly delightful in every way. Smart, sweet, pretty; the whole package.

I don't quite get my son's need to keep things from us. In this crazy world, every bit of nice news is welcome. My older sons eventually learned to share their news with me and I hope in time my youngest will as well.

Until he does though, I will continue to stalk as necessary, because a mom's gotta do what a mom's gotta do. However, my husband has learned his lesson and has retired from stalking.

CIA BOY GRADUATES

Youngest son sent us confirmation that he will indeed be graduating this upcoming weekend, having completed all the requirements for his degree.

In the screenshot he shared with us, I noticed that, in addition to his major in math, he also completed a minor in Near Eastern and Judaic Studies. Wait, what?

He was in school for four years and never mentioned the minor.

At least this child of mine has been consistent. Although I paid a king's ransom for college, I know very little of what actually went on there. Occasionally he would throw me a bone and send a picture or tell me some small thing that had happened, but I knew that was a mere drop in the ocean and that there was waaaay more he WASN'T telling me. I did know he was mostly happy and that was good enough. As you know, being the mother of three sons, I've learned not to expect too many specifics. In fact, if they go into too much detail about something, my brain gets confused. When I speak with their significant others however, I get the complete opposite. So. Much. Detail. Famine or feast.

Back to my youngest son. I want the CIA to know that he's been a stellar operative. No secrets were revealed, and the USA remains safe. If an agent can go four years without mentioning what he's studying, he should probably be promoted. I also suspect that all those times my child said he was playing video games online with friends, he was actually practicing tactical maneuvers for the agency.

In any event, I think that my son will go far in both of his careers, the one at the brokerage company I know about and the one I'm pretty sure I know about.

I can't wait for graduation.

MY IT GUY

My IT GUY (also known as CIA Boy, and a recent college graduate) is back! Thank heavens, because my husband and I have been (metaphorically) sitting here in the dark for the past four years.

Despite the fact that before he left for school, our considerate son created a lengthy Google doc outlining what to do in case of various technology emergencies, from time to time we still find ourselves a little lost.

I mean, while he was away at college, I missed my son because he's a pleasant person and all that, but let's be honest. People my age do better with someone in the house who grew up with computers and phones that weren't rotary.

For example, the cell service in our new house isn't great. So our son ordered something from the phone carrier called a booster and then spent last night setting it up. Lo and behold, our cell service works better. Mr. Aisle 4 and I would have continued saying, "Excuse me, I didn't hear what you said" while talking on our cell phones for the rest of our days or until we moved again, whichever came first.

While glancing at my cell phone, IT Guy muttered something about my apps not being in folders. He might as well have been speaking Klingon but I will let him organize my phone—I suspect it will be a big improvement.

It's not that Mr. Aisle 4 and I are old. Actually, it is that we are old. Which really isn't our fault. At least we were smart enough to space our children far apart so that we would have tech support for decades. By the time IT Guy moves out, we are hoping we will have grandchildren who will be able to help us.

When hubby and I decided to have children, we thought about things like passing on our values and producing people who would someday become productive members of society. Never mind about any of that. We now realize the most important reason to have offspring is so that when your internet goes out, you have someone to fix it.

THE HOBBY I THOUGHT I NEEDED

My youngest son got his girlfriend a Wooble for her birthday. What is a Wooble you ask? It's a crochet kit where you make adorable little creatures by watching videos.

A good friend of mine had told me about them— her son purchased one and seemed to finish it in no time at all. (By the way, this is not a sponsored post and the Wooble people are not paying me.)

I decided to get myself a Wooble too. I figured I could use a new hobby and this seemed like the perfect one. I ordered Pierre the Penguin. My son's girlfriend has Fred the Dinosaur.

For the record, my son didn't think I would enjoy Woobling. What does he know, right?

My Wooble arrived and when the girlfriend received hers we started Woobling together. Meanwhile, she has taken to this project like a duck to water and I hate it. Like loathe it with every fiber of my being.

First of all, my hands shake so it's difficult for me to complete the stitches. And I'm really bad at following directions. My mind wanders and I forget where I am. There are all these new terms like "increase stitch" and some other stitch and I get them confused. My son was right and Woobling is not for me.

I'm so ready to quit. For the record, there is no shame in quitting things. In fact, if there is something you feel like quitting, I give you my blessing. Cut your losses and move on.

However, the girlfriend won't let me. She said if I get to a certain point she will finish it for me. She keeps telling me I can do it. While I appreciate her support and enthusiasm, I disagree. I can only do it while she sits next to me and guides me. Which means I only work on Pierre when she is here visiting my son. While she is almost done with Fred, Pierre looks like a small yarmulke. He's a long way from being done.

I've begged her to take Pierre away but she will not. I already see the type of mother she will be. No enabling there. I admit at some point I just did my kids' homework for them in the interest of sanity (my own). I can tell you, when this young woman has kids she will not be doing their homework. She will be telling them how bright they are and how they can do it on their own. Awful, right? I don't know what my son sees in this person.

Meanwhile, when she isn't here, I keep Pierre in a drawer so I won't be reminded that I'm not working on him.

At the rate I'm going, I will have completed this project in the year 2027. Or later. I promise to post pictures if and when he is ever done.

Lessons learned:

1. Don't be suckered into buying things from ads on the internet.
2. Listen to youngest son. If the CIA hired him, he must be smart.
3. Quitting things is fine.
4. Handbag shopping is the only hobby I need.

PIERRE THE PENGUIN—FOLLOW UP

When last we spoke of Pierre the Penguin, he was just a small blue disk that looked like a kippah. I had pretty much given up on him. Until...

The girlfriend came to visit this past weekend. And she was a little bored. So, she picked up Pierre. I think she couldn't help herself. When she sees a Wooble she instinctively wants to pick it up and start crocheting.

I am happy to report that, except for his tummy, Pierre is almost done. I would say she did half. Okay, maybe 65 percent. FINE—she did like 90 percent of him. But I affixed his eyes and sewed on his beak. I'm much better at sewing than I am crocheting; I had two great aunts who were seamstresses who taught me how to sew. If a button falls off your shirt, I'm your person.

Anyway, the girlfriend asked me if she could keep Pierre for her collection. If you know me, you know that I am a generous person. I love to give gifts. But I cannot give away Pierre.

He needs to sit on my night table reminding me to make good choices in life and not be swayed by ads. Even though he and his Wooble friends are too cute for words, they aren't for everyone.

We will never speak of Pierre again, but I wanted to let you know what happened with him in case you were wondering.

I always told my kids that if they learned something from an experience, even if it didn't turn out as expected, it was valuable. I've decided to take my own advice.

DORM ROOM DECORATING: BOYS VS. GIRLS

My youngest son's girlfriend is visiting this week ahead of going back to college in Massachusetts. Rather than fly back to the East Coast with a ton of stuff, she's had some things delivered to our house—including bedding.

We started chatting about her comforter, which is cream colored. She mentioned that she had been concerned that the cream wouldn't match the white throw pillows and other accessories in her room.

I must've had a dazed look on my face during the conversation, because she asked, "Didn't you want your dorm room to look nice?"

Of COURSE I wanted my dorm room to look nice. In fact, I wanted a rainbow comforter in the worst way. Back in the day, everyone had a rainbow comforter. But my mom took me to Burlington Coat Factory where an ugly, dark green comforter with a forest theme was on sale so we bought it. Needless to say, my side of the room was never going to be featured in a magazine unless it was in an article titled "How Not to Decorate Your Dorm Room."

(By the way, by my junior year I bought myself that rainbow comforter, which I used for the next twenty years. After college, I kept it near my bed for naps or just as an auxiliary blanket for when I was cold. I only threw it out after all the stuffing was coming out and it could no longer be mended.)

The reason I had that dazed look on my face was because not one of my three sons cared about their dorm room. And not one of them cared about their comforter. At all. When we went to Bed Bath & Beyond (may its memory be for a blessing), I chose all their bedding which was some combo of gray and navy like all the other boys' rooms which were decorated by their moms. Not only didn't my sons not care about their bedding, they didn't care much about anything else.

When my youngest son moved into his dorm room, I tried to get him to hang posters on the walls but he was even opposed to that. I've seen prison cells which looked cozier.

He did care about his electronics and WIFI—he was logged in and playing video games within seconds of arriving at school.

Even though I'm a female, I'm sometimes taken aback by female talk because I've spent so much time with boys that my brain needs a little rebooting.

Once again, it's not that girls are better than boys. Or boys are better than girls. They just prioritize different things plus their brains are not wired in the same way.

For the record, I happen to think a cream-colored comforter with white throw pillows is perfect.

MINI GOLF WITH MY FAMILY IS ALWAYS A HOLE-IN-ONE

Every summer we go mini golfing. By "we," I mean me, my husband, and whichever kids are around. It's been a tradition since my sons were little—we even take an annual photo with Pinocchio (who used to be on the fourth hole but now is on one of the holes on the back nine).

I didn't think we would get there last summer, but on Labor Day, when my youngest son asked us if we wanted to meet him at the mini-golf place, I jumped at the opportunity (even though I was tired and it was ten thousand degrees outside).

Of course I was happy to spend time with my youngest son, but I also happen to enjoy mini golf. There aren't many sports I can play (yes, I am calling mini golf a sport and if you disagree, please keep it to yourself) because I have a bad back and hips and knees and I don't like to run or throw things or catch things. But I CAN do mini golf. I may not be the best at it, but at least I compete.

There are definitely some holes I find more challenging than others. Like the one where you have to get the ball in the volcano-like structure in the middle. I hate that hole—the ball just keeps falling back down and it makes me feel like Sisyphus. However, on most of the holes I can putt par. (I think that's how you say it in golf lingo.) I sometimes even get a hole-in-one. When that happens, I all of a sudden know how professional athletes feel when they get a home run or touchdown. Okay, maybe that's a wee bit of an exaggeration but you get the idea. For a brief moment I am not sucking at something that involves a ball.

I've never won a free game but I'm sure it's only a matter of time until I get that ball in the clown's nose. Despite nearly getting heat stroke yesterday, I had a lot of fun. And although I didn't win, I did not come in last place either.

MOM 2.0

Today is my daughter-in-law's birthday. I signed her birthday wishes "Love you, Mom 2," which is sometimes how I refer to myself with her.

It was actually her Mom 1 who came up with the moniker several years ago when we were wedding dress shopping and the sales associate asked who I was. Mom 1 and Mom 2—sort of like Thing 1 and Thing 2 but without the blue hair and red jumpsuits.

Over the years I've discovered that as Mom 2, I have an important role to play. Sometimes it might be as a stand-in when Mom 1 is not available but more often it's a completely independent role.

I've known my daughter-in-law for more than eleven years and during that time, we've developed our own relationship. A bond which is part mothering, part friendship. I'm the one she comes to when she needs an explanation of how my son's complicated brain works. Or when she needs an opinion on a handbag (handbags are my jam). And I go to her for things too—she designed the covers for my books, and since she works for Meta, she's an excellent resource for my blog and all things Facebook. She also teaches me about all the girl things I had no idea existed.

I admit that I have occasionally felt pangs of jealousy over the close relationship my daughter-in-law has with her mom. She will be the first to acknowledge that she's obsessed with her. I know we can never have that. Because I didn't raise her. I escaped all that fun teenage girl angst. But then I get over myself and realize how lucky I am and that what we have is pretty good. And I do have a dog who is obsessed with me so there's that.

I've learned that being a mother-in-law to girls is not always an easy gig—in fact, it can sometimes be a little tricky. But it's a role I've come to love. Because the young women my sons have chosen as partners make it easy.

Cheers to all of us Mom 2s. We are lucky ducks for sure.

PART-TIME PARENTING IS MUCH EASIER

My oldest son came home yesterday—he went to a Phish show last night in Hartford, Ct. and our house is on the way.

He doesn't come home that often anymore—he's married and has a demanding job. Although he only lives about an hour away in Brooklyn, it sometimes feels as if it's further. But he's happy so I'm happy.

Anyway, I picked him up at the train and we headed over to the mall. Prior to arriving, he had asked if I wanted to go clothes shopping with him and I had said yes. I'm not big into sports so there aren't many things over which I can bond with my sons.

We probably hadn't been clothes shopping together in years. I helped him choose slacks and shirts and then sat outside the dressing room while he tried things on. I offered my opinion on how things looked and he actually listened. Although we went during the store's big anniversary sale, of course nothing we chose was on sale.

I must admit that it was a really pleasant hour or two. When we got home, he went for a run before heading out for the show. Figuring he'd get hungry, I packed him dinner—a tuna fish sandwich with lettuce and tomato on whole wheat. I cut up carrots and threw in a banana and some chips as well. Since it was a thousand degrees, I made sure to include ice packs in his little cooler.

I made sure he had a blanket to sit on for the outdoor show and enough cold water for the car ride.

He returned from the show at 1:24 am. I know this because I was half-listening for him to come in. Which is a habit I've never quite been able to break.

By the way, my child is 30 years old. A fully responsible adult. But his age doesn't matter much; he's still my kid and I still like to take care of him.

I'm fully aware that if I were back to parenting my three sons 24/7, yesterday would not have been so much fun. Duh. Back when it was full-time, it was overwhelming My boys seemed to outgrow clothes and sneakers faster than I could get to the stores. They always needed something. And the food thing—OMG. If I missed a day at the grocery store, the employees worried about me. It was never ending. Until it ended. (Except for the pandemic when they were all around but that was an aberration.)

That's the thing about parenting. It's kind of all or almost nothing. It would have been nice if things could have been a bit less intense while they were growing up.

So, when I tell one of them, "I was just thinking about you", it's the truth. For today, tomorrow, and always.

But that's not how it works. So you have to muddle through the thick of it and savor the thin of it.

I might run to the store and get some more of that tuna fish he really liked.

GOING BACK IN TIME

The other day I was in a store trying on a jacket. I wasn't sure which size to get, so I asked a woman who looked like someone whose opinion I could respect.

She was younger than I am, I'm guessing fortyish. And I'm sixtyish. Yikes.

Anyway, she supported my decision to get the bigger size. I tend to like bigger. While chatting, she mentioned she had three sons between the ages of three and ten. I mentioned I also had three sons, ages 21–31. And three almost daughters as well.

Right now her life is about being in the middle of the chaos. And I'm at the point where being a full-time mom feels like a lifetime ago. Actually, three lifetimes ago.

Would I want to be her? Hmmm. Maybe for an afternoon. To feel needed, to be a total part of my boys' lives, to snuggle with the three-year-old and read him bedtime stories. But not full-time. I just don't have the stamina. I sometimes marvel at how I ever did it at all.

Would she want to be me? Hmmm. Maybe for an afternoon. To have freedom and not worry about school pick up, playdates, homework, etc. But not full-time. Because she has to go through all the hard and wonderfulness first. I mean, she doesn't even have a teenager yet! She hasn't sat in the passenger seat (expecting to die at any moment) while her child learns to drive. She hasn't seen her sons fall in love.

I thanked the woman for her assistance. She walked me to my car, and I gave her copies of my books, which I keep in my trunk. I figured she might find some advice in the pages which could help. Or at least get a laugh or two.

After we parted ways, I thought about life a little bit. How slow and fast it all goes.

And I felt grateful to be exactly where I am now.

OUR KIDS REALLY ARE PAYING ATTENTION

Last night my youngest son mentioned something that I had never told him but had written about on Aisle 4. (I think it was about having first seen the movie *Hair* in Canada.)

It was an insignificant thing but it was proof that CIA Boy DOES read my blog. Aha!!

Realizing he had been busted, he said that he only read it because he was bored and, for good measure, added that he doesn't read it all the time.

Too late. The truth was out.

This was just further proof that our kids really do want to know what we have to say. They are totally paying attention even when they want it to appear that they aren't. Which is why we need to keep talking even when we think the conversation is one-sided.

Now that I know for sure he's reading my words, going forward I plan on including subliminal (and not so subliminal) messages in my blogs and book chapters. (Which is perfect for someone in the CIA.) Please clean your room, empty the dishwasher, walk the dog, and especially, I love you and am so proud of you.

Because that's the most important message of all.

I WAS JUST THINKING ABOUT YOU

The other day when my son called, I said to him, "I was just thinking about you!" Later, I thought about what I had said. And I realized I was probably always thinking about him (and his siblings), whether I realized it or not.

Of course, I think about them when they call or text. Or on their birthdays. Or when I need technical support. That's when they are front and center of my thoughts.

But the rest of the time, they are in the not-so-far recesses of my mind, easily accessed. I think about them when I walk past their empty rooms and when I'm in the grocery store and see their favorite foods. Or hear a song they like. I think about them when I see a young mom with her child in a stroller, remembering how we used to be. I think about them when I see a school bus or see kids playing basketball at the hoop near our house where they used to play. And  I think about them when the house is quiet at night, hoping they are all okay.

The way things are going
I feel like it's time to
use the good dishes

~Thoughts From Aisle 4

PART 2: MOVING: IT'S HARDER THAN IT LOOKS

MAKING THE DECISION TO MOVE

*B*ack in 1998, we were living on Long Island in a small, three-bedroom split level family house. Hubby (before he became known as Mr. Aisle 4) commuted to the city daily and I was busy raising our one, and then two, active sons.

My brother-in-law and sister-in-law had been living near us but then decided to move to Westchester, about an hour north of the city. They told us about a new development near their new house and brought us a brochure.

We looked. And we liked what we saw. But it was expensive. And Westchester was a foreign land. Not foreign like a different continent but not what I was used to. I'm not great with change. But I knew we would outgrow our little house. My younger son's bedroom was more like a closet, and he looked like he was going to be big (he's 6'2" so that prediction turned out to be correct).

I also knew that moving gets harder as kids get older. I moved in fifth grade, which was manageable, and then again in eleventh grade, which was impossibly hard and lonely for me. I do not recommend it.

So, with a loan for the down payment from my brother-in-law and sister-in-law (for which I am still grateful), we bought a house in that new development. We were the first ones to move in—we were pioneers like the Ingalls family. Okay, maybe not exactly but there was no cable for the first month we were there. Just ask any mom with two young sons how difficult that can be. Anyway, we adjusted. And it was good.

Because everyone was new to the neighborhood, we all bonded. There were block parties, and Halloween became a huge thing, with hordes of trick-or-treaters flooding our neighborhood. Every year on the night before the first day of school, a bunch of us would have dinner together by the community pool. We carpooled and watched out for each other's kids.

As time went on, people started to move away. As people tend to do. Some moved out of state for jobs. Some wanted bigger houses. Some people decided they didn't want to live in a community with an HOA (homeowners' association).

I was content. I called our house a mansion because to me it was. I started out in Brooklyn and the Westchester house was bigger than anything I had known before. We had FOUR bedrooms. As a child in Brooklyn, I shared a room with my brother.

But the pandemic changed a lot of things. And I changed too.

I got older and crankier. I loved some of my neighbors. But others, not so much.

There was the nosy neighbor who patrolled the streets like Mrs. Kravitz on *Bewitched*. And the neighbor who reported people who left their cars on the street overnight (a $25 fine in our HOA). We had the guy with the red truck who kept a MAGA hat on display on his dashboard, although he eventually put it away.

They put up speed bumps that were more like hurdles. My husband's low-to-the-ground electric car scraped bottom every single time we went over it. In fact, much to his dismay, a piece on the bottom of his car fell off. It must not have been an important piece because the car still works. But we saved the piece just in case.

And then came the pickleball. That was the beginning of the end for us. Actually, the beginning of the end was when our next-door neighbor's air-conditioning unit started to die. It still cooled, but it made a horrible grating sound. And it was loud. And drove us crazy. People would walk by and ask what the noise was and I would yell, "It's from NEXT DOOR!!" It got fixed after a year or so, but we never fully recovered. I learned that certain types of noise can actually be traumatizing.

Back to pickleball. Our house was located next to the community pool and clubhouse. There was a tennis court and playground as well. We knew what we were buying into when we purchased our house. There was some noise, but it never really bothered us. I actually enjoyed the occasional sound of kids playing and splashing.

A few years after we moved in, the kids on the block (including mine) wanted a basketball hoop. The HOA told me if I got everyone within earshot of where it would be situated to sign off on it, we could get one. So I got the neighbors closest to the clubhouse to sign a form and we did indeed get a hoop. What does this have to do with pickleball you ask? I'm getting to that, trust me.

Sometime during the pandemic, a neighbor went down to Florida and discovered pickleball. I've played a few times and it is indeed fun, although the pivoting hurts my back.

ANYWAY, the neighbor decided we needed a pickleball court. Two in fact. And since she was on the HOA, no forms or sign-offs were needed. So, they put lines on the tennis court and voila! Overnight we had pickleball in the 'hood.

Fabulous, right? Only not so much. Two courts, often four people (some of whom didn't even live in our 'hood) on each court.

Pop. Pop. Pop. Pop. Pickleball is ridiculously loud. The constant noise broke me. For the record, I'm not anti-pickleball. I'm just anti-pickleball all day long next to my house.

I could have raised a ruckus about the courts and the constant noise. But I just didn't want to. I was weary. I knew it was time to go.

Yes, I sold my house and moved two miles away because of pickleball. But not really. It's never just one thing.

Our house, which I loved in many ways, which was the longest place in which I had ever lived, sheltered us from many storms. I was grateful to that house for so much. I knew it so well I could navigate it in the dark. Before we got our generator I had done just that.

I miss the family with whom we sometimes did Havdalah. I miss our neighbors with the little white dog. I miss the across-the-street neighbor who I would remind to close her garage door at night. I miss my good friend and walking buddy even though she has walked here at the new house with me many times. I miss the older couple with the amazing garden who let us take our son and daughter-in-law's pandemic wedding pictures there. I miss other people too. And our dog Maisy misses her friends Charlie, Gus, George, Cash, Nola, Bodhi, Pepper, Yankee, Cody, Jimmy, and so many others.

We are currently living in an unfinished house. It will be done eventually. It will be beautiful. Someday. We will have a first-floor master bedroom. When they build it. Dealing with a builder has been an interesting and frustrating experience. But that's another chapter.

Sometimes change is necessary when you're feeling stuck. Even though it can be hard.

May you find a way forward when you need to.

FINDING YOUR DREAM HOME

So once you decide you want to move, finding a new place to live should be easy peasy, right? Absolutely wrong.

You have to kiss a lot of house frogs before you find the right one. And even when you find the right one, it's still never going to be perfect. Because there's no such thing as perfect. That goes for everything—houses, significant others, handbags, etc.

Mr. Aisle 4 and I made a list of the things that were most important to us in our next house and started our search. What was on that list? As I mentioned, a first-floor primary bedroom was key. And we wanted to stay in the same town. Now that my kids are grown, I like it here even more than I did years ago. Good restaurants, a wonderful grocery store and coffee shop, nice people. Plus I have friends here. And our temple isn't too far away.

We also didn't want to be in an HOA. We were so over the whole HOA/rules thing. And I couldn't be within a mile of a pickleball court.

We needed a house that could accommodate our growing family when they came to visit, and something a little more private than our previous house. A good view was high on my husband's list—our old house had a small but wooded backyard. It had been the perfect spot for a pandemic wedding. (But that's another book.)

After two years of looking, we found a house about two miles away from where we were that was on a small lake. It was a house built in 1938 that a builder purchased with the intention of gutting and flipping. So to be clear, we did not hire this contractor. He came with the house, like the geese and stink bugs.

We knew the house had drawbacks. For example, the first-floor ceilings were only eight feet high. (Apparently people were shorter in 1938.) Since we are somewhat vertically challenged, we figured that would be okay. The garage is detached—we were told that building a covered walkway between it and the house would not be difficult. Of course it's a way bigger deal than we were led to believe.

This turned out to be a huge project. Much larger than anticipated. The house needed everything. In hindsight, it would have probably been a better idea to knock down the existing house and start from scratch. Honestly we had no idea what we were getting into or who we were into it with.

I did ask around about the contractor because I was leery about him, but the people who knew him said he seemed congenial enough. However, none of the people I queried had done business with him. I had 34 mutual Facebook friends with his ex-wife, and the builder and I seemed to know a lot of the same people. I should have checked him out more extensively. I should have driven out to the Hamptons (where he said he had done most of his work) and actually looked at projects he had completed and spoken to his customers. I should've looked into his past businesses. Should've, would've, could've. Bottom line, we didn't do our due diligence. Big mistake. Huge.

As I said, no house is perfect. If you get most of what's on your wishlist you're in good shape. Only you can decide what's a deal breaker. And what isn't a deal breaker right now could become one in the future. But what's most important is knowing who you're doing business with. Let the buyer beware and all that.

I've thought about other houses we came close to buying. And what we could have done differently to have avoided the unfortunate situation in which we found ourselves.

But as we all know, there's no going back. There's only learning from your mistakes and moving forward. And in my case, since I'm a writer, helping others learn from my mistakes.

Our small lake is indeed pretty. And a first-floor primary is not overrated. We weren't wrong about those things. And as for the rest? We will make it right. And when we are done, this will hopefully be the house we imagined when we set out to find our dream home.

I've reached my quota
for being annoyed this
week so if you're planning
on irritating me you're
going to have to wait

~Thoughts From Aisle 4

TIME TO USE THOSE NEW TOWELS

A few months before I moved, I bought a bunch of new towels. Someone had given me a gift card and it seemed like a perfect use for the found money.

Our old towels still worked—I mean, they dried us after a shower. Which is the purpose of towels. But they were frayed, and the brown color wasn't my favorite.

Since our new primary bedroom isn't finished, I hadn't used the towels. I was waiting for it to all be perfect before I broke them out.

The way things are going, it's going to be a while until that bedroom is habitable. It's not even sheetrocked yet.

As I mentioned, one of the reasons we moved (besides escaping the pickleball noise) was so that we could have a first-floor primary bedroom. My back and hips, Mr. Aisle 4's knees—My father, who was a master chess player, always taught me that it's important to plan ahead. We are okay now, but we anticipate that at some point in the future a first-floor primary will come in handy. And it's a good thing we started ahead of time because who knows how long the construction will take. I might be collecting social security by the time we are in that first-floor bedroom.

So I made an executive decision and broke out the new towels. And I'm using them while we are living in one of our kids' bedrooms upstairs. I gotta say, these light gray towels are nice. Soft, pretty to look at. A big upgrade from the old brown ones.

Sometimes it's important not to save things for the future. Sometimes getting pleasure in the now is the right thing. And while I'm waiting for the contractor to get his act together, I may even go out and buy some new sheets.

GEESE—WHO KNEW? (NOT ME!)

The house Mr. Aisle 4 and I bought/built/renovated is located on a small lake/big pond. And on this small lake are geese. Which are charming to watch.

A few months ago, the geese on our lake had babies. And let me tell you, you've never seen such amazing parents. I don't know how much parental leave they get, but it seems endless.

The adult geese NEVER leave their babies. Not for a single second. In addition, there are always four grownups tending the group. One in the front, one on each side, and one in the back, making sure no one gets lost or left behind. It takes a village, right? I love how the goslings are raised communally. By the time the babies leave, the parents will have earned some much needed rest. Maybe somewhere south, like Florida.

Anyway, now that I've said something nice about the geese I am going to tell you how they are driving us insane.

Let's start with the fact that we had no lawn. So we paid a landscaper a tidy sum to bring in truckload after truckload of dirt, grade our property, and then seed. The geese family love to eat the seed. I get it; the moms are probably sick of hearing, "What's for dinner?" and our seed is like dining out. However, we want a lawn. So we yell at the geese like crazy people. "Get out of here." "GO AWAY!"

Like. Crazy. People.

Which we kind of are at this point. A year ago we could pass for normal folk. Not any more. This house thing—I can't even.

Interestingly, our rescue pup Maisy, who barks at anything that moves, does not bark at the geese. I think she feels sorry for them. Or perhaps is afraid of them.

Anyway, not to be defeated by geese, my husband ordered an anti-geese spray. Which they loved. Yum. Next he ordered air horns. Which are making us deaf. The geese don't like the sound and they do run away when they hear it. And then they come back, scoffing at us all the way. We also have cap guns which are fun to use but similarly ineffective.

I have run outside in my bathrobe yelling at them to stop eating our almost lawn, but they are even less afraid of me than my children were. I gotta work on being more scary.

In addition to the fact that I really want a lawn, the geese poop everywhere. It's totally gross. One time decades ago, when we were watching my oldest son play soccer, my younger son ate goose poop. He was probably around 20 months old at the time and nothing happened to him, but I still have PTSD from that incident.

Next year, we will start the battle against the geese a lot earlier in the season. We will try new methods. And we will prevail. Maybe.

NO GOING BACK NOW

Before I moved to my new house, I worried. "What did you worry about?" you ask.

Well, lots of things. But this piece is about the fact that, after 24-plus years in my old house, I worried I would miss it.

That house was where I raised my three boys. The house where I measured my sons' growth on a wall. The only house in which my youngest son had ever lived. The house which sheltered us from a pandemic. The backyard where my oldest son and daughter-in-law got married during said pandemic. (It was amazing by the way.) What kind of monster was I to leave a house which held those memories??

We sold our old house in one day. And when we signed the papers, I was gripped with panic because I knew there was no turning back.

The new owners seemed very nice, but I thought it was unlikely they would want to live with me if I changed my mind. I'm not a morning person and can be kind of grumpy before my coffee.

And then there was my husband who happened to be one of the most nostalgic people I had ever met. What if he regretted it?

Turns out, even though our new house became a building nightmare, neither my husband nor I miss that old house. What we felt in our gut, that it was time to move on, was right.

Since we moved within the same town, we can still see the neighbors we liked. We took that growth wall with us. And if our kids ever want to show their kids where they got married, the backyard will still be there.

We have a nice relationship with the new owners who let us know when we have mail or packages. (It is ridiculous how long it takes for mail to stop going to a former residence.) And every time I've pulled up to my old house, I haven't felt a whit of regret. In fact, I've felt certain that we made the right decision. I am so glad that fear did not hold me back.

I am not telling you what to do. If you decide to move and it turns out to be a bad decision, I don't want to be blamed. I don't want that on my conscience.

I am only telling you about my experience. And the fact that I am a big believer in trusting your instinct.

By the way, my new contractor, and his crew (aka the cavalry) showed up this morning to resume construction on my new house. This first day of spring is feeling like a new beginning.

THINGS THAT GO BUMP IN THE NIGHT

Just when I thought I wasn't going to have much to write about today...

The people who lived in the house before our builder bought it just stopped by. A lovely mom and daughter. The daughter asked me if I had heard any noises.

Noises??
Yeah on the steps. Or at the top of the steps.
Um, no.

She said that when she was a kid, she used to hear someone walking on the stairs. There was a cold spot on the landing as well. But they performed an exorcism and the exorcist told the ghost to cross over to the other side. Not the other side of the street—the BIG other side. Like at the end of the movie *Ghost*, when Patrick Swayze goes off to heaven.

And apparently our house ghost did just that. (By the way, the former owners believe it was a male ghost—possibly a former gardener.) However, the daughter mentioned that she was worried that all the construction might have stirred him up. Or brought him back. Or something. I'm not exactly sure how it works.

I'm actually more afraid of builders who scam the living than I am of ghosts who haunt. And if there is a departed spirit here, so far he's left us alone. Maybe he feels sorry for us and figures we have enough on our plate.

In addition to *Ghost*, I love the movie *Beetlejuice*—I learned a lot about the afterlife from it. I know that most ghosts are friendly. They mean us no harm. But I'm really glad the previous owners warned us, just in case.

The mom and daughter were also here to see their old copper fireplace which they said our builder had promised them he wouldn't touch. I was sorry to be the one to tell them that, like the ghost, the fireplace was gone. But they took the news in stride and the mom said with a philosophical shake of her head and shrug of her shoulders, "Builders…" Yeah.

If I see the gardener ghost I will let you know. And I will be sure to ask him if he wouldn't mind doing some landscaping for the free room and board. Sounds fair, right?

BREAKING UP (WITH YOUR STUFF) IS HARD TO DO

This post is for anyone who is considering moving in the next few years. Or the next decade. Because if you're anything like me, it might take you a while to get ready.

Before I moved this past December, I knew I had to get rid of stuff. I had been in the same house for almost a quarter of a century with the same husband and three children and I, no WE, had accumulated a lot of stuff.

So last summer I started purging. And I honestly thought I was being pretty good about it. I opened every closet and drawer and when I peeked inside I pulled out a few non-essential things to toss or donate. Yay me!! Only, not so much.

We got to our new house and started unpacking. Because our house was still under construction, we really couldn't unpack that much. So we lived with a lot of boxes all around us, waiting for the day when we could finally finish putting everything away.

Well, mates, that day finally arrived. And I am properly horrified. I brought clothes I hadn't worn in years. Much of which was pre-Covid and pre-menopause. Which means most of it doesn't fit. I brought single socks without partners. Did I think the missing socks would be waiting for me at the new house?? There was expired medication, and lots of arts and crafts made by my children, only one of whom has any artistic ability.

The arts and crafts thing is tough. There are things that were made by my sons' small hands, decades ago. Before they grew up and got snarky. Like the menorahs they made in nursery school that have bolts to hold the candles. What kind of terrible mother throws stuff like that away?? I realized I needed to be that terrible mother.

So I sent them pictures and asked if it was okay to toss them. And with their permission I did just that. Okay FINE. I admit it. I saved one of those menorahs (I'm not going to tell you which one). I'm a work in progress.

Let's talk about bedding and towels. I had mismatched pillow cases and old duvet covers as well as threadbare towels that honestly aren't even suitable for our dog. How many towels does a family actually need? Probably two for each person. I had dozens. Which was a habit handed down to me by my mother and grandmother who had closets stuffed with old towels. Like you would open the closet and towels would fall out and bury you. I finally realize it's up to me to break this chain of hoarding old towels. Yes, Mom, I realize if there's a flood in the basement I might need some extra old towels—I have enough in case that happens so please don't worry.

We have bags and bags of stuff to donate. Bags and bags of stuff we brought out to the curb. And stuff I haven't gotten to yet. I'm trying to be methodical and mindful as I unpack.

Even if you're not moving, it's not a bad idea to start getting rid of things. Which means emptying each drawer and closet, not just peeking at the top layer as I did. Deep purging requires time, effort, and hardening your heart. I've taken pictures of some of the things I've tossed but that only helps a little. Once things are gone, I know I will forget about them and not even miss them, but in the moment it's difficult.

So, mates, the moral of this piece is don't be like me. You're welcome.

And now I'm going to go open another box.

I want to be a minimalist
but I like stuff too much

~Thoughts From Aisle 4

GUTTERS—THE UNSUNG HEROES

Due to circumstances beyond our control, we moved into a house which had no gutters.

Which did not seem like a big deal. To be honest, I had never thought a lot about gutters. I mean, we had them at our old house and once a year I paid someone to clean them, but that was pretty much the extent of it.

Turns out, gutters are more important than you might expect. Who knew? (Probably everyone but me.)

The word gutter derives from the Latin gutta which means "a droplet" and they were invented around 3,000 BC (bet you didn't know that).

In the three plus months we've been living here, we've had a lot of rain. Like an insane amount— we've hardly had two days in a row without some precipitation. And many of those rainy days included downpours of a biblical nature. We even lost power during one of the deluges.

Each time we had heavy rain, a moat formed around our house. OHHHHHH—so THAT'S what gutters are for!!!

The moat thing was interesting. It was suggested to me that we build a drawbridge. And maybe get a few alligators. However, I have a smallish dog and I've heard that alligators are known to eat smallish dogs, so that wouldn't be good. Plus I'm not sure where our town stands on alligators—they have a lot of ordinances, so I'm guessing alligators would be a no go.

I never thought I'd be writing about how excited I am at the prospect of getting gutters. A new handbag? Yes. Gutters? Not so much. But life is funny like that.

The gutters will connect to things that connect to drywells that are somewhere under our lawn. Or something like that. I'm not entirely sure how it works. But I do know that the gutters will solve our moat problem. And I cannot wait. THIS IS THE WEEK WE GET GUTTERS!!!!!!

I want to give a shout-out to all the gutters out there—unsung heroes that are pretty much ignored. But never again by me. Going forward, each and every day I will be deeply grateful for those gutters.

Our Moat

DON'T TELL ANYONE, BUT I LOVE DUMPSTERS

When my original builder (of not-so-blessed memory) departed, he had the porta-potty that was on our property removed. Which was fine because there was no chance I'd ever use it. I'd sooner pee in my pants. However, he left the dumpster they were using. It's on our front lawn.

You need to understand that I totally love dumpsters. I am being serious. I've been asking my husband for one forever. ("Can I please have a dumpster for Hanukkah?") So this is like a dream come true. Got some rancid food? Throw it in the dumpster. An old broken piece of furniture? Dumpster. Dog poop? You get the idea.

I don't even mind that it's sitting in front of my house. It goes with our current décor which is Mid-Century Mess.

Having a dumpster is a constant reminder that I should be purging. It motivates me to reassess all the crap that's in my house. Realistically speaking, I know I'm never going to be a minimalist because I like stuff too much. Put it this way: there are always things in my Amazon cart.

Years ago when a friend was renovating and told me she had a dumpster, I was green with envy. But now I have one of my own. Sometimes good things really do come to those who wait.

I realize that the dumpster is not a permanent situation and someday our house will be done (we are very close to hiring a new contractor). And when our house is completed, we will probably need to get rid of the dumpster. I hope by then I will have used it to the fullest and gotten the whole dumpster thing out of my system. But who knows? I imagine I will probably feel a little sad when they take it away.

But that day is not today. Today is ripe with possibilities of how I can use my big, beautiful dumpster.

GEESE: PART 2

I've told you about our geese situation. So I thought I'd update you just in case you ever find yourself with the same problem—geese who poop everywhere and mock you.

Let's review the things that don't work:

Goose Stopper Spray. False advertising. Doesn't stop them at all. Doesn't even slow them down. Returned to Amazon.

Air Horns. Does make them flee. Temporarily. And then they return. Meanwhile you've gone deaf. No more air horns. My ears are still ringing.

Cap Guns. Super fun to shoot. Love the smell and the popping noise. Like being a kid again. Same effectiveness as air horns (although less likely to cause hearing loss).

Yelling and chasing them. Just makes you look ridiculous.

Something that does work:

Fencing. Mr. Aisle 4 installed deer fencing around bushes. Geese went through the bushes. Put fencing around the bushes. No more geese. For now we have won the battle. Not sure about the war. At some point we will have to install a real fence.

One thing I will say about my husband and myself. We don't give up easily. You should know that about us just in case. In case what? I don't know—in case you ever have to deal with us. We are super nice people, but persistent. Like fungus.

Have I mentioned that our AC has been broken? For a week. Yes, one of our two units is kaput. After eight weeks of use. How is that even possible? I know things don't last as long as they used to, but eight weeks? Meanwhile the guy who was supposed to fix it would only talk to my husband. Yes, that is still a thing. I kept telling him I have complete agency to deal with such matters but he kept asking me when my husband would be home from work. Obviously, that did not go well for him. Some men are just such jerks. I want to use a stronger word but I won't because this is a G-rated book.

Anyway, if I sound slightly off balance at the moment, well, it's because I am. Tired, frustrated. And have a headache from the heat. Sigh.

At least the geese are leaving us alone at the moment.

KEVIN AND FUTURE LANDFILL

Before I moved, I did a poll regarding whether or not our ginormous stuffed bear Future Landfill (FL) and our rather large carnival-won minion Kevin (from the movie *Despicable Me*) should come to our new house with us.

Overwhelmingly, my readers said yes to keeping FL and no to Kevin. So, I threw out Kevin and I was proud that I had done so because purging is hard for me.

Meanwhile, my husband, in an effort to find his shoes, was out in the garage at our new house rummaging through thousands of boxes of stuff and found Kevin.

I was like WTF???

He WAS in a trash bag but somehow that bag made its way to our new house.

Since Kevin cheated death, my husband didn't have the heart to throw him away a second time. So now he's in the bonus room above the garage sitting on a couch with the TV remote living his best life.

BOOMERANG MUG

My husband dropped off a college travel mug which said "Proud Brandeis Parent" with a bunch of other stuff at a thrift store in our town. We decided to jettison it because we had too many mugs, not because we aren't proud parents or don't love the school.

A friend spotted the mug on the "for free" shelf at the thrift store and grabbed it for me.

Another prime example of why becoming a minimalist is just so darn difficult.

Me: I don't need anything

Also Me: Ooh, an Amazon Prime deal

~Thoughts From Aisle 4

BEWARE OF THE CRAPPY CONTRACTOR

Yesterday one of my readers messaged me asking for the contact information for the lawyer we are using for the lawsuit against our Terrible, Horrible, No Good, Very Bad Contractor. (Sorry—that was one of my kids' favorite books and I couldn't resist.) She also wanted the name of my second contractor. The one who actually takes pride in his work and finished our house.

She told me a little bit about what she has been going through and it sounded awful. My heart went out to her and anyone who has been gaslit by an unscrupulous contractor.

I suggested at the very least she hire an independent person to oversee the work. If there is a foreman on the job, he doesn't have your back. He has the contractor's back because that's who he works for. They are in cahoots. I wish someone had told us that before we began our project. Someone needs to write a book called, "Here Is Everything You Need to Know Before You Even Consider Building or Renovating a House." A long title but I personally happen to like long titles for books.

I know that many of you are thinking, "You're a writer. You should do it." More than a few people have messaged me privately and encouraged me to make this book a what-not-to-do-when-you're-building-a-house guide. And while I appreciate the confidence in me, I don't think I could write an entire book about this topic. I am happy to have a few chapters about it; however,

I find the subject matter rather depressing. Not like Holocaust depressing, but not amusing either. And I prefer to make people laugh, at least some of the time.

Why do contractors mess up so often and so badly? The obvious answer is that it's easier to cut corners and cheat. Because you make more money. But in the end you really don't. Tortoise and Hare. Another classic story.

I don't believe in the concept of heaven and hell. But I do believe in honesty. If I just made stuff up all the time you guys would know. And I would feel icky. I understand that many people don't feel icky when they lie. But ultimately lying catches up with you. It may take a while, but it does. And then you have the reputation of being a big fat liar.

I've given out the name of my second contractor several times. He's a good guy who does solid work. So yeah, if you live in my corner of the world and need a solid contractor, I've got one for you.

Just remember, before you embark on any renovation, BEWARE.

UNPACKING (OR DO I EVEN REMEMBER WHAT'S IN THE BOXES?)

Yesterday Mr. Aisle 4 and I tackled the basement boxes. It was a perfect day for it—rainy and humid and we had nothing else on the agenda.

There were three things I could have done with the boxes.

1. Toss them all out without opening any of them. We've been in this house for seven months (time flies when you're living through construction hell) and I really didn't remember what was even in the boxes. Some were vaguely labeled (books, frames, etc.) and some weren't. I figured if I hadn't missed what was down there, how important could any of it be?

2. Ignore them forever. Simply pretend they don't exist. Boxes? What boxes?

3. Open each one and sort through the contents.

We opted for number 3.

I am happy to report we tossed a lot. Garbage day is going to be another banner one here at chez Fischer. I plan on tipping our sanitation workers handsomely this Christmas.

Anyway, we went through pretty much everything. Hubby and I disagreed on some stuff—like old letters we had written each other summers when we were in college and living at home in different states. I was ready to toss; he wasn't. And there was some stuff I just could not say goodbye to: The little music box I got when I was five, the index box with the addresses of people we invited to our wedding and the gifts they gave us, a large framed photograph of my grandmother. I figure that when we are gone, our kids will have no emotional attachment to any of it and will be able to toss it all easily which is fine.

I did get rid of the Cliff and Monarch notes I used in college and had given my kids when they were in school. Remember those? They were supposed to be used as supplements, although some people used them instead of actually reading the books. I think they are available online now—no need to save.

It was a trip down memory lane for sure. Perhaps someday in the future we will be able to toss more, but for now I'm satisfied.

We arranged the remaining boxes neatly and I swept out the storage area.

Next up: The garage where we stored the rest of our stuff. Now that I know I can do it, I hope the task will feel less daunting.

TOILET PAPER HOLDERS WITHOUT SPRINGS ARE A GAME CHANGER

On Saturday I went looking for stuff for my new primary bathroom at a plumbing supply store. I was a little overwhelmed by all the options for toilets and tile and whatnot.

But I was also surprised and delighted to discover that in the category of toilet paper holders they had very few with the spring inside. You can still get them but honestly, with all the other choices, why would you? (Unless you have a masochistic streak in which case you have bigger problems than toilet paper.)

I thought to myself that, if they disappear altogether, future generations might never know what it was like to try and put a new roll of toilet paper on the holder, only to watch the spring shoot across the room. In addition, the noise of all the parts of the holder falling to the floor, especially in the middle of the night, was a little too jarring.

I admit that in the past, I was not great about changing the roll. And this is one of the reasons. In our new house, all the toilet paper holders are the newer kind, the ones without the spring. They simply lift and it's delightful. They also make ones where you slide the toilet paper right onto the holder. Any two-year-old or teenager can do it. I'm not sure if my husband has noticed that since we moved, I've been better about putting a new roll on the holder. After almost 36 years of marriage, I am finally pulling my weight in this area.

I realize in the grand scheme of things toilet paper holders aren't all that important. And although I wouldn't call the newer ones life altering, I would say they are a definite upgrade. Actually, I take that back. They are indeed life altering.

I'm not suggesting that you swap out all your toilet paper holders today. That's a lot of effort for a Monday. But if perchance you happen to need one in the future, know that you have choices.

GEESE: PART 3

They're baaaack. Yes, I'm talking about those pesky geese.

As you know, our new house came with a gaggle of geese. Which we spent much of the spring/summer trying to get rid of. We tried various methods. Including a fake coyote (decoyote), which only managed to scare my middle son.

About a month ago, the geese disappeared. Mr. Aisle 4 thought it was because he had finally succeeded in chasing them away with paintball guns he had borrowed. I figured they had joined my mother-in-law in Florida for the winter. I mean, their kids had grown up and they probably needed a vacation.

However, yesterday afternoon I saw them again hanging out by the lake. I almost didn't have the heart to tell my husband because he had made it his life's mission to make them go away. But I figured he'd see them sooner or later, so I broke the bad news to him during dinner.

Right away, he asked me if I had shot (near, not at) them with the paintball guns. Seriously? I'm the person who didn't even like our boys playing with toy guns.

So of course I told him that I had actually purchased a high-power rifle and instead of turkey we'd be having Canada goose for Thanksgiving. With all the usual sides of course. I realize that hubby has had it with those geese. But I will not be arming myself in any way to address this issue.

Maybe the goose family went to Florida and returned North to visit some relatives or have a family reunion. Perhaps they missed us. Who knows?

In the meanwhile, I'm a little concerned that my spouse, who I've known since I was 17, thought there was any possibility that I would use those critters for target practice. I'm going to chalk it up to a momentary lapse in sanity. Which I get.

I feel like since we won't be spending much time outside during the winter months, perhaps we can all coexist. At least until spring when the feud is likely to begin again.

IS MY WEDDING DRESS ACTUALLY IN THE BOX?

After I got married almost 36 years ago, I paid what for me was the exorbitant price of $150 to have my wedding dress cleaned and preserved (whatever that means). I had no idea what I'd ever do with the dress but for some reason I thought this was a good idea.

When I picked up my dress it was (allegedly) sealed in a box inside a bigger box. Which I never opened. Every time we moved, that big box moved with us. From time to time I wondered if the dress was actually in there (that's the Brooklyn skeptic in me). Then I'd assume it was (that's the optimist in me) and go on my merry way.

A few nights ago, I was discussing wedding gowns with my middle son's fiancée. And in that moment I just had to find out if the dress was really in the box. So even though it was late, we went and got that big box from the room above the garage which has been its most recent home. And together we opened it.

Inside the outside box was a treasure chest with a cellophane front where you could see inside—like a Barbie box. And lo and behold, there was my dress. And veil. We unpacked it and held it up.

My first thought was, "Wow, was I ever that skinny?" I still love the dress's raw silk material but oh my, those puffy sleeves!!! What were we all thinking with that style? Even Princess Diana had those sleeves on her wedding dress. So 1980s.

There was no way that gown was getting any further up my body than my knees so my almost daughter tried it on instead. She looked so pretty in it. I have no illusions that my dress will ever be worn again but it was nice to see it. Sort of like visiting with an old friend and taking a little trip down memory lane. By the way, if you can still fit into your wedding gown (and weren't married in the last five years) you have my respect.

We carefully repacked the dress and at this moment it's on my dining room table. I will probably put it back in a storage room where it will stay until I figure out its fate. Which will most likely be to continue taking up space wherever I live (that's the sentimental side of me).

These past few months I've been working on purging things and overall, I feel like I've done a pretty good job. I even tossed a small foosball table that my brother and I played with when we were kids. I admit I shed a few tears as I added it to the garbage heap but it was time. You don't need things to preserve memories.

But sometimes you need to hold on to a preserved dress for a while longer.

LESSONS FROM MY NEW HOUSE

So, what have I learned? Here are a few takeaways.

To start with, I will never build a house again. I guess never is a long time so I will amend that to I will not build another house in the next thousand years. Maybe 950. People have said it's like childbirth and you forget after the pain is over. However, decades later I still remember the pain of my three C-sections. Not saying it wasn't worth it, but I definitely haven't forgotten.

Will I still trust people? Yeah, probably. Even though I'm originally from Brooklyn, which comes with built-in cynicism, deep down I want to trust people. I'm a very honest person and I am always confused by people who aren't. Like, how hard is it to just be honest? (Apparently very hard.)

Misogyny is alive and well. Even among men who have wives and daughters. Because it's easier to call a woman crazy than own your mistakes. Just effing own it.

I am not alone. The number of people who have had issues with contractors is astounding. I've gotten more comments about this topic than anything I've written in a while.

There are still people who do fabulous work. Like the kitchen guy I used for my old house. As the kitchen was being done, I never had to point out an imperfection. They saw it before I did. And fixed it. I was spoiled by this guy. Someone who cared about his reputation.

I'm also trying to learn patience. This will all get done, somehow, eventually. And I'm learning to live in a house that's a huge mess. When I can't take it anymore, I either sit in my youngest son's closet, which is totally organized, or go out. I guess it's nice that at age 59 I'm still learning. That's a positive.

Most importantly, I still have my sense of humor. And when I laugh at the absurdity of all of this, I know I will be just fine.

Being part of a family means encouraging each other, comforting each other, enjoying each other, and even tolerating each other—but always, always, loving each other

~Thoughts From Aisle 4

PART 3: FAMILY & FRIENDS: THE RELATIONSHIPS THAT GROUND ME

MY GRANDMOTHERS

I was extremely fortunate to have grandmothers for as long as I did. Between the two of them, they taught me everything I ever needed to know. About being a wife, mom, woman. And although they are no longer here, they remain within me.

NEW GRANDMA

I had the opportunity to spend some time with my youngest son's girlfriend's sister, mom (who I had met before), and grandmother. All lovely. But especially special was her grandmother. To see the bond they all have with "Tata" as they call her reminded me of my relationship with my own grandmothers whom I loved so very much.

We called my dad's mother New Grandma. She was born in Hungary and left the country after World War II. Her husband had been gassed to death in Auschwitz; she also had been in the concentration camp but managed to escape. My grandmother was allowed to leave Hungary because her son, my dad, had already emigrated to Canada.

When my grandmother left Canada and moved to New York where we were, my older brother didn't really know her. So he called her the "new" grandma and the name stuck. At least I think that's the story. For a long while, I thought her name was one word: Newgrandma. My other grandmother would sometimes call herself the "old" grandma, but we will get to her later.

New Grandma wasn't a huge fan of New York. And when her sister moved to Florida, she happily followed. Boy, did she adore Florida! She truly appreciated the flowers, warmth, and sunshine. It was her paradise and she made me love it too. My brother and I would visit her every year, sometimes with our parents and sometimes without. Generally, my brother was the favored child because he was The Boy. But in New Grandma's house I got the bigger bedroom. With my own bathroom. Because I was The Girl. How cool was that? When I visited her when I was in college, she even gave up her bedroom for me. At the time, I don't think I really appreciated how nice that was.

I will never forget how special my grandmother made me feel. She used to stare at me a lot. I thought it was kind of odd behavior, but I accepted it. When I became a mom, I understood it. She stared at me because she couldn't get enough of me.

I remember New Grandma trying to teach me how to cook when I was a little girl. She showed me how to crack an egg and then had me try it. Unfortunately, my egg landed on the floor instead of the pot. (Perhaps it was foretelling of my future culinary abilities or lack thereof.) A little worried she would be mad at me for making a mess, I looked up at her only to find her laughing. Phew. She liked to laugh and that was a good thing.

New Grandma could be a little crazy, but she was also fun. She was always up for anything—she took me to the mall, jai alai, the dog track (she loved to gamble), and out for pizza. Pizza was both of our favorite food. My grandmother was a little obsessed with food. When I woke up in the morning, she literally demanded to know what I wanted for dinner. I get it now—food doesn't prepare itself and she needed some lead time.

Every year when I said goodbye to New Grandma, I worried that I wouldn't get to see her again. 89, 90, 91— She did have a stroke when she was 89, but even though she was in a wheelchair she kept going. 96, 97, 98...

New Grandma's last few years were spent in a nursing home. I took my sons to visit her and even though she seemed a little out of it, she rallied enough to note my handbag and my oldest son's ripped jeans. I assured her that the ripped jeans were a fashion statement and not a result of my spending too much money on the handbag.

A few months before New Grandma turned 100, we had a small celebration for her. I presented her with a note I had procured from the President. There was cake and, yes, pizza.

I called her on her actual 100th birthday but I could tell something was wrong. I do think she knew she made it to 100. Later that day she went into the hospital, and she died four weeks after that.

She might have liked to be buried in Florida, but we flew her up to New Hampshire and buried her next to my brother who had died ten days earlier at age 48. We never told my grandmother that my brother was ill, and I imagine she was pretty surprised when she got to heaven and saw him there.

I always say that I hope I have more than a little bit of her genes in me because she was a strong lady. And even though she didn't have much of a formal education, she was super smart. I often watched her add sums lightning fast and was impressed. Although my dad was a staunch Republican, she was a Democrat. She wanted things to be more equal in this country and I loved her for that. I remember her saying that the rich people would take all the sunshine for themselves if they could. But luckily everyone could enjoy sunshine.

Olga Klein Kohn Kerenyi
April 29, 1908 – May 29, 2008

NANNY

When I was growing up, my family always lived with my mom's parents. First in Brooklyn, in a two-family house. Next in Merrick, Long Island with my grandma and grandpa downstairs, and then, just my grandmother in our home in Nashua, New Hampshire.

Nanny was born in Poland in the early 1900s. Maybe 1902? We don't really know because they didn't keep great records in Poland. Plus that side of my family didn't like to talk about age. It was a SECRET.

My Nanny was one of five girls. And she was fiercely devoted to those sisters. She and her older sister Molly (for whom I'm named) came to America fleeing pogroms and poverty. They worked hard to bring their other sisters and mother out of Poland as well. However, by the time they had enough money, the United States had closed its borders. So the rest of the family ended up in Montreal, Canada, which was the closest place to New York they could go to. We remained very close with our Canadian relatives, traveling there every year for Passover. And they visited us whenever they could. My grandmother used to say that if she did nothing else in her life, at least she got her family out. She was so proud of that.

Nanny was a very gentle person. I rarely saw her angry. Mostly just at my grandfather for smoking and eating things that weren't good for him. And she was the most selfless person I've ever known. She gave and gave to me and my brother, as well as every charity that asked. She had keychains from a million organizations to which she had donated. I learned the importance of philanthropy from her.

When I was in my teens, I spent every Friday night in her den with her watching TV. We both loved the CBS lineup that included *The Mary Tyler Moore Show* and *The Bob Newhart Show*. And when we were done watching I would kiss her goodnight and she would say "Make the light" so I wouldn't fall when I went upstairs. "Make the light"—I still hear those words when I turn on the light to go upstairs for the last time every evening.

I also hear her admonishing me when I do laundry on Saturday, which is the Jewish Sabbath. "You have to do wash on Shabbos?" Sorry Nanny. I also hate to travel anywhere by plane on Saturday for the same reason, although I still do it.

A deeply observant person, my grandmother followed the rules of Judaism as best as she could. She disliked eating in restaurants and never ate much more than a baked potato when we went out. Things regarding religion were much more loosey goosey on my dad's side of the family.

Although my grandmother didn't have a career, she always stressed how important it was for a woman to be able to make her own money. Both of my grandmothers told me that. Nanny helped fund my college education and I think that she would be proud that I'm finally doing something with that education, albeit a little late in the program. I wish that my grandmothers could have seen my name on my three book covers. The only person in my family of origin who got to read my published words is my mom.

As I mentioned earlier, Nanny had no idea when she was born. I was probably around ten when I realized that the rest of us had birthdays but we never celebrated hers.

So I picked a random day in July and every year after that we celebrated her birthday on that date. She professed not to care, because she never wanted it to be about her, but I think (hope?) she was secretly a little pleased.

My grandmother wanted everything for me and my brother and my mom. And nothing for herself. It still amazes me. To be loved like that—is everything.

Gertrude Brandt Sapsowitz
July 24, 1902 – November 23, 1999

**To everyone who prayed
the volleyball wouldn't come
anywhere near them in gym
class—you are my people**

~Thoughts From Aisle 4

True friends don't worry
about whose turn it is
to call. They just pick up the
phone and start complaining
where they left off.

~Thoughts From Aisle 4

COLLEGE FRIENDS GETAWAY

Recently, I mentioned that I was going away with a group of my college friends for the weekend. So I'm guessing you're wondering: How did it go?

Well, the short version is that it was wonderful.

When you are together with people you've known for over 40 years, it's kind of magical. And beyond comfortable—like slipping into your favorite pair of worn sweatpants.

What did we do during the weekend? Well, we ate a lot. And did some drinking. We walked around the town. And sat around and chatted. We moved from couch to couch in a pack.

We even had matching sweatshirts like people wear at Disney. Which made us easy to spot; when I was looking for my friends in town, without me asking, a woman said, "Your friends went that way." Matching sweatshirts are key. Perhaps it looked like we were escapees from an assisted living facility but that's okay.

There were some frank discussions. We talked about the horrible situation in Israel and Gaza and the antisemitism in this country. And of course we are all on the same page.

We talked about things we might have done differently in our lives. One theme for a lot of us was that we would have been more mindful in choosing careers. The young women today seem so much better at figuring out what they want to do and at juggling careers and families. I wish I had kept writing. But I also recognize that times were different—working from home wasn't a thing. Laptops weren't a thing. I've been trying to make up for lost time but beginning again in my fifties wasn't the easiest.

Back to the friends weekend. On a personal note, I do not sleep well in hotels. In fact, it's a little bit of torture for me. The first night after finally falling asleep at an ungodly hour, I was woken up by some device on the night table at 7 a.m. Even after I unplugged it, it kept beeping. So I buried it under a mountain of pillows. The next night before going to sleep I made sure it was not plugged in. But it woke me again, and because of the time change it was at 6 a.m. Super annoying. I suggested to the front desk that they throw it off a balcony in deference to the next guest.

When we said our goodbyes, I felt a tug at my heart. Because it had taken us so long to do this weekend, I have no idea when it will happen again. But I think that we are committed to not waiting as long. Seeing each other for a day is great, but being together for an entire weekend was even better. It nourished my soul.

My grandmother Nanny was wise in a lot of ways; however, she believed that friends could never take the place of family. But this was one of the few times she was wrong because my friends ARE my family. I am truly blessed.

SUPPORT GROUP FRIENDS WHO STILL SUPPORT

Last night I mentioned to my youngest son that I was going into the city today to meet a couple of friends.

He asked, "Which friends?" I said they were old friends he didn't know. He pressed on and wanted to hear more about them (for someone who literally tells me nothing he wants a lot of info).

I explained that these two women had been part of my dead baby group. For some reason that pretty much ended his inquiries.

Thirty-four years ago, after I lost my first son to a congenital heart defect ten days after birth, I joined a bereavement group. Which was one of the best things I ever did. Although I had some extraordinary friends, they hadn't been in that awful situation. Most of them hadn't even been pregnant yet.

That group meant everything to me. It was a place where I could pour out my feelings and not be judged.

After the sessions officially ended, some of us stayed in touch. I spoke with one of the women every single day, for hours. I knew her voice so well that many years later, when waiting on a security line at the airport, even though her back was to me, I heard her speak and ran over to hug her. She worked for an airline and my kids thought I had lost my mind and was hugging a random employee because I was so happy to be taking a vacation. (Which I probably was.)

When this friend gave birth to her second daughter I was thrilled for her but also a little sad because I knew she'd be too busy for our daily chats. Lo and behold, she called me as soon as she got home from the hospital. That phone call meant more to me than I can express.

Anyway, I am happy to report that we all went on to have other children.

I was pretty excited for our lunch because it had been a few years since I had seen one of them and decades since I had seen the other.

I wanted to hear everything about their lives. I also wanted to know how those losses so many years ago affected them. One of my friends observed that the kind of trauma we experienced stays with you. After our babies died, none of us were ever the same. I barely remember the person I was before I lost my first son. I experienced my first panic attack while he was undergoing open heart surgery—at that moment my low-lying anxiety became full blown and I've been trying to beat it back ever since.

We learned in the most painful way that life can change in an instant. We all still worry about what bad things could happen next. At the same time, we agreed that our losses made us more grateful for the blessings in our lives. Gender preference for children (and now grandchildren) is a luxury none of us can afford. We all understand that any pregnancy that ends with a healthy baby is a miracle.

Despite many ups and downs, my friends seem like they are in a good place. Being together again made me happy.

I usually like to end my stories with a tidy little bow. But sometimes life isn't tidy enough for a bow. Just good people who are there when you need them.

LESSONS IN GRIEF

As you know, 34 years ago, I became a mother for the first time. Although my son lived only ten days, I think it's fair to say his brief life changed me forever in ways I am still trying to understand.

> I learned for the first time (but not the last) that catastrophe can strike at any given moment. That vigilance won't always protect you. That the ground you thought was solid can suddenly shift and open up and that you can fall into the abyss.

> I learned that there are good people who will help you climb out of that abyss. They are often (but not always) people who have known loss too.

I learned that you are often stronger than you think.

I learned that life is about getting up again, even when you think it may not be possible.

I learned that you can heal. (But some scars will remain.)

I learned to take nothing for granted.

I learned to be grateful and count my blessings.

I learned to laugh (a lot) and feel joy again, and to appreciate every happy moment.

I learned that even when someone you love is gone, they will always be a part of you.

I learned to help others climb out of the abyss.

I learned we don't want the people we love to be forgotten.

A few months after my son died, I received his social security card in the mail. When I got it, I stared at it for a long time—I felt as if that small official piece of paper somehow made his short life more real. But over the years, I learned that I didn't need a government document to validate his existence. The love I felt and the lessons I learned were more than enough. His life did indeed matter.

In memory of Jared Michael Fischer
March 24 - April 3, 1990

GOING ON AFTER THE UNIMAGINABLE

Yesterday my cousin in Hungary sent me a photo of our grandmothers and their sister taken in 1948, three years after World War II ended.

All three women had been recently widowed, their husbands sent to the gas chambers by the Nazis. My grandmother had also been in Auschwitz but managed to escape by running into the forest during a forced march. She often told me how she had come face to face with the notorious Dr. Mengele, who for some reason decided she would not be among those sent directly to the gas chambers. Maybe it was because she was young and pretty? Who knows? Mengele, also known as the Angel of Death, performed sick "medical" experiments, often on twins—I will spare you the details. She described him as a handsome man with piercing eyes. But he was pure evil—the devil incarnate.

My grandmother (the one in the middle) and her older sister (on the right) would leave for Canada shortly after this picture was taken; my father and his cousin had already emigrated there with other children who had lost parents during the war. The third sister, who was pregnant at the time, was not allowed to leave Hungary—I don't know how long it was until they saw each other again. I can't imagine how they all felt.

I was struck by the fact that in the picture they are smiling. How were they able to smile after all that had happened?

My grandmother would start a new life in Canada and then again in the United States, ultimately retiring to Florida as I mentioned in an earlier chapter. And despite the fact that she and her sisters quibbled constantly, they remained fiercely devoted to one another. I remember she and my great-aunt, who also retired to Florida, talking on the phone all day long. They never said hello or goodbye; they just kept the conversation going. And when their younger sister visited from Hungary, they were overjoyed. They would all proceed to fight and make up, fight, and make up, but they were happy.

How does one become so resilient? Are you born that way? Can you learn to be strong? Is it a combination of both? My grandmother's older sister used to say, "The life is no good. The people are no good." She was a little dark—with good reason. Yet she still could laugh and be silly. My grandmother never forgot what happened but yet I would say she managed to enjoy her life and appreciate every little thing, every little bit of sunshine that came her way.

I think the three young women in that black-and-white photo made the decision to go on and they did. And not just survive, thrive. Every bit of happiness was an eff you to those who tried to destroy them. Or maybe it wasn't so much of a conscious decision to go on, just something that was within them. I know that having each other and their children helped a tremendous amount.

In times when I struggle, I think about all of my grandparents and what they went through. And even though they are gone, they still give me courage, strength, and faith.

YOM KIPPUR

At sundown this Sunday night, Yom Kippur, the Day of Atonement begins. This is the holiest day of the year for Jews and includes prayer, fasting, asking for and granting forgiveness, and introspection.

On this day, we also remember our loved ones with a special prayer service, called Yizkor.

While at services yesterday, I started thinking about those who are no longer with us and how we remember them. There was a specific reason for my train of thought.

The details are a bit murky to me, so if I get some of this wrong, please forgive me. My family has been members at our temple since we moved to this area almost 26 years ago. There was an older gentleman who attended services regularly. And during one of the prayers he would get up and dance, with members of his family. And the Rabbi too. Even as he grew frailer, he was there, doing his best to participate and be joyful.

My kids referred to him as Grandpa Mikey. I believe he wrote a children's book that he read to them during Hebrew school.

Anyway, Grandpa Mikey passed away a number of years ago. His family still attends services at my temple. And during that particular prayer, the Rabbi joins them for a little bit of dancing.

That's how it is with those who are no longer with us. Actually, that's incorrect. They ARE still with us—we just have to work a little harder to see them. They appear on cue and also when we least expect them. During a song, a joke, or a moment which we know they would have loved. Or hated.

If we allow them, they are there to offer advice or just to listen. From time to time, I say a word or two to my brother, who died 16 years ago when he was just 48. And sometimes, even though I'm in a hurry, I stop to turn off a light that has been left on because I can hear my dad saying, "Are we supporting the electric company?."

Although we can no longer have their physical presence, the people who are gone from this earth can still offer us many things. And if you look closely, you can see them dancing joyfully to a special prayer.

As we get older
whatever kind of
weird we are
only gets weirder

~Thoughts From Aisle 4

**Good friends listen
politely when you repeat
a story and pretend they
haven't heard it before**

~Thoughts From Aisle 4

Falling apart isn't
so bad as long as
you have good friends
to fall apart with

~Thoughts From Aisle 4

PART 4: GROWING OLDER: I WAS HOPING TO AGE LIKE FINE WINE BUT I'M FEELING MORE LIKE AN AVOCADO

GROWING OLDER WITH FRIENDS

*T*here are a lot of reasons you need good friends. But I've decided that one of the most important reasons is so that you have people to get older with.

Hear me out. Imagine you started falling apart while your friends stayed perpetually young. How awful would that be? It simply would not work.

It's okay to have a FEW younger friends but you really need to surround yourself with people who speak your language—the language of the decrepit. For example, when I call a good friend who is around my age, we can discuss which body part is currently giving us the most problems: shoulder? knee? hip? neck? back? And it doesn't end there.

We talk about how little we've slept, how tired we are, which new medications we've added to our morning/evening routine, which doctor appointments we have coming up, etc. While the conversation might not be scintillating, it's certainly comforting and, honestly, even somewhat amusing. What we lack in estrogen and collagen, we make up for in self-awareness and humor.

In addition, none of my friends want to stay up too late. If we actually happen to go out together, we are happy to do it on the earlier side and then call it a day. I couldn't have friends who wanted to start the party at 10:00 p.m. I would last five minutes. Maybe not even.

I don't believe that youth is wasted on the young. My kids seem to know exactly what to do with their youth, and good for them. I'm okay with where I am now. Mostly. Once in a while I wish I had the mediocre energy I had when I was younger. But then I give thanks to the aging gods for not being harsher to me.

BEDTIME ROUTINES

Before we go to sleep, my husband washes his face (with our pump hand soap), brushes his teeth, and puts in his eye ointment. The entire process takes under three minutes.

I am fascinated by this because my bedtime routine has about 67 steps that can take anywhere from 20–25 minutes to complete. To skip a step or two would be to invite catastrophe. I could end up with drier or oilier skin (I have combo), more wrinkles (if that's even possible), etc. Who knows what else could happen but I'm certainly not about to find out.

Obviously, packing for a trip can be difficult. In fact, after I pack my toiletries, I really do need a vacation. I have travel sizes for some of my potions and lotions and hair products, but not all. So I store them in multiple pouches and then, invariably, I run out of room in my suitcase. Since I have a very kind husband, he usually lends me real estate in his bag. (Young ladies, marry a guy who will share his suitcase. Trust me on this one.)

As I've gotten older, my bedtime routine has gotten longer. I can only imagine what will happen if I live to be 90. Either I will have to start getting ready at around 2 p.m., or I will have to give up. In which case, I will just wash my face with hand soap, brush my teeth, and call it a day.

LIKE AN AVOCADO

A few weeks ago I was in Florida. After a very dreary few months here in New York, I was happy to see the sun and feel warm again.

Feeling invigorated, I decided that I'd be a new, healthier me. Yay!! So every day, Mr. Aisle 4 and I took long walks on the beach. I love the beach and I love walking. Win win.

Only not so much. By the end of the week, my feet started hurting. When I got home, I could barely walk without serious pain in my heels. What fresh hell was this?

I googled my symptoms (what in the world did we ever do without the internet?) and discovered I have something called plantar fasciitis. Yikes!

Although I walk two miles every day with my rescue pup Maisy, I think walking barefoot on the hard sand used different muscles. Sigh.

I've been icing, stretching, taking Advil, and wearing cushioned pads on my heels but they still hurt. Especially the left one. At some point I may have to go for physical therapy. I haven't been there since my sports bra shoulder injury. When I said goodbye to my therapist, I told him "So long for now." I knew that I'd be back eventually; it was inevitable.

I think I need to point out that the last two injuries I've had were because I was trying to engage in physical activity. I'm sensing a pattern.

My mother-in-law, who is fabulous at 91, never exercises. As in never has, never will. In fact, when I've tried to get her to take a walk with us, she's gotten hostile. I'm thinking that she might be onto something.

I probably should've stretched before those long walks on the beach. But I've taken many long walks on sand in my life without any dire consequences.

That's the thing about aging—your body changes. It often doesn't like the things it used to. And it's not shy about letting you know.

I'm not exactly sure what my point is. Don't move? Or if you move be aware that you could be risking injury? That cannot possibly be a moral to a story.

Maybe there is no moral. Just a suggestion that you stretch your calves and ankles before heading out for a walk on the beach.

And now I'm going to hobble into the kitchen and get some ice for my heels.

ROAD RAGE

The other night, my husband and I went out to dinner. On the way home, we were stopped at a red light behind a red sedan. When the light turned green the red sedan didn't move. After waiting an appropriate amount of time—long enough that even I asked why the red sedan wasn't going—my husband tooted (not honked, tooted) his horn.

The guy in the red sedan waved his arm for us to go around him. I figured he was having car trouble or perhaps he was answering an important text.

As my husband drove around him and started to make a right turn, red sedan guy moved forward and almost hit us. I figured it was just a mistake.

But then, red sedan guy started chasing us down a winding road. My husband sped up and did a fine job not getting us killed in the process. But red sedan guy was hellbent on catching up to us and he did.

After nearly rear ending our car he zoomed past us and I thought "phew." Until he stopped short in an apparent effort for us to hit him.

I went from scared to petrified. So I dialed 911. They told me I was calling 911 in the wrong town and would connect me to the right town. Which they didn't. It took three tries to get us to the town which we were in (who knew calling 911 could be so difficult?!).

I explained our emergency and road rage red sedan guy. Being in a semi-dead zone, the call kept going in and out.

I heard one dispatcher say to another that a female in a car was being chased. The second dispatcher asked if it was a young woman to which the first guy answered, "No, it's an older woman."

Wait, what? Older woman? Forget road rage red sedan guy. How could they tell I was older? Do I sound older? I'm only 58 for goodness' sake! I didn't call anyone sonny. I didn't say, "Excuse me while I put my teeth back in my mouth." I'm in the prime of my life, aren't I?!?!?!

Eventually road rage red sedan guy stopped terrorizing us and, after giving us the finger for what seemed like several minutes to show who was boss, he turned off onto a side street.

I've decided I will never toot my horn at anyone ever again. If I'm stopped at a light behind someone who doesn't move after it turns green, I will take out a book and read until they decide it's time to move. I will sit there all day if need be.

There are a lot of unhinged people out there. Be careful mates. And for those of you who have heard my voice, do you really think I sound like an older woman?

Never mind my car,
I need an extended
warranty for my body

~Thoughts From Aisle 4

I'm at the "Oh look,
there's a bathroom –
I probably should stop
in and pee" stage of life

~Thoughts From Aisle 4

KEEPING IT REAL

I was with my big kids recently when they got a notification from an app called BeReal. They hurriedly took a picture of what they were doing at that moment and posted it. Since they are young and adorable, pretty much everything they are doing looks fun.

As the name implies, BeReal is supposed to be a less posed/filtered/fake social media platform than, say, Instagram. The point is not to be perfect.

It occurs to me there should be a BeReal specifically for people in my age group. Maybe it could be called ALittleTooReal or BeRealPlus.

The in-the-moment pictures might include us middle-agers at physical therapy trying to unfreeze a shoulder or working on a knee, back or hip issue. There might be photos of us dozing off because we didn't sleep well the night before. Or maybe wandering around a parking lot clicking the beeper thing because we can't remember where we left our car.

I imagine myself posting shots while getting my hair colored, tweezing an errant chin hair, or wearing reading glasses while I try to read a label in the grocery store.

Now that I think about it, ALittleTooReal might not be such a great idea. The pictures might be scary and there would need to be a warning: "The photos you are about to view are graphic. Viewer discretion is advised."

I'm guessing I won't be getting a job in app development any time soon.

I love to play a game
called "Guess what's in
the package because
I can't remember what
I ordered." It's really fun.

~Thoughts From Aisle 4

THE CAMEL LOAFERS X2

A reality of getting older is that you forget things. Words, appointments, the name of that guy who was in the movie you really liked with that blonde woman with longish hair.

When it happens I just chalk it up to the fact that I'm no longer 25 and move on. But sometimes, it can be a little alarming. Or a lot alarming.

Case in point: The camel loafers.

Last October I saw a pair of camel suede loafers with shearling inside that I really liked. But they were over $300, and honestly, I didn't need them. So I did the responsible thing and passed on them.

But January was a big bummer of a month with both Mr. Aisle 4 and me sick for basically its entirety. So I decided to treat myself to those loafers, which were still on my mind. I was delighted when they arrived.

BUT—When I went to put them away, I saw the same exact camel loafers on the shelf in my mud room.

What???? How did they get there? I admit that I started to freak out a little. And I wondered if there was something seriously wrong with me.

I called the store and spoke to the sales associate and asked when I had purchased the first pair of loafers. She looked up my sales history and said I had bought them on November 19. In other words, I'd had them for two months and hadn't even noticed them in their box on the shelf.

After my initial panic, I decided to think more deeply about the situation and how the loafer situation could have occurred.

November 19 was the week of Thanksgiving. Which I hosted. And whenever I host, even if it's only eleven people, I get stressed. In addition, and here's the more important part, my grandson was born on Thanksgiving and my daughter-in-law was in early labor that entire week.

So I'm guessing I bought the loafers, put them on the shelf, and promptly forgot about them because I was super distracted. That's my story and I'm sticking to it.

Of course I asked a few good friends if I seemed okay to them. Because, despite my reasoning about how I could have bought the exact pair of shoes twice, I was still concerned. I got assurances from them that I seemed fine as well as stories of their own memory lapses. In fact, I told this story to one friend at lunch and after we paid she asked our server if she had paid. I thought she was just pretending to forget as a kindness to me but no, she actually hadn't remembered handing over her credit card.

I think that as we age, our memory banks fill up. And in today's society we are paying attention to too many things at once. Like our cell phones. We tend not to focus on one thing at a time. I find that writing things down and making lists is helpful in my quest to remember.

The moral of the story is that, next time I see something I like, I'm just going to buy it straight away.

Lol, no. That's not the moral. I'm just going to try and pay closer attention to what I'm doing. And when I forget something, chalk it up to one of the joys of aging.

Oh by the way, I started wearing those loafers and am loving them. (And yes, I returned the second pair.)

One day you're young and
fun and the next you're
pissed off because you
left your kitchen reading
glasses in the bedroom

~Thoughts From Aisle 4

TURNING 60

Here's a little conversation that's been rattling around in my brain.

Me: I don't want to turn 60.
Also Me: What are you talking about?

Me: I've decided I don't want to turn 60.
Also Me: Seriously? You're the one who always says it's just a number. And it's better than the alternative. Etc.

Me: I know. I'm a hypocrite.
Also Me: Birthdays never bothered you before. Why this one?

Me: I'm not sure.
Also Me: You know you have readers in their 70s, 80s, and 90s who will scoff at 60.

Me: Yes, I realize that.
Also Me: Just think of all the good things you have to look forward to: a grandbaby (G-d willing), the house being finished...

Me: We are blessed for sure.
Also Me: So?

Me: I just don't want to get any older. I'm already falling apart. And 60 just sounds yucky.
Also Me: So call it 59 plus.

Me: Very funny. As our kids like to say, you're not being helpful.
Also Me: I don't know what you want me to do.

Me: I guess just listen.
Also Me: Okay, I can do that.

Me: You know I will get over this. As soon as our birthday passes I will forget about it.
Also Me: Memory loss is a definite sign of aging.

Me: Again with the jokes.
Also Me: That's how we cope.

Me: Yes. It's our default setting.
Also Me: Yup.

Me: Well, thank you for being here for me.
Also Me: No problem. And happy almost birthday.

Me: Happy almost birthday to you too.
Also Me: We are going to be fine.

Me: Yes we will.

I used to envy people who could do a cartwheel but now I'm jealous of anyone who can get up off the floor without making grunting noises and holding onto the furniture

~Thoughts From Aisle 4

**Me: This is a password
I will never forget**

**Me three seconds
later: Crap**

~Thoughts From Aisle 4

TAG TEAM RECALL

Every so often, my husband or I will say something like "What was the name of that person?" and the other one of us will say "Which person?" and then one who initiated will have to explain a little further. "The person who lived on the corner of that street we just passed when we were driving home," or "The title of the movie we saw with Susan and Michael twenty years ago," or "The tall blonde woman who used to live in our neighborhood—you know who I'm talking about—the one who got divorced and moved to Florida."

I call this game Tag Team Recall. Tag Team Recall requires two players, generally middle-aged or older, who know each other pretty well and understand the way the other person thinks. You can play anywhere because you don't need a board or pieces, just a slightly addled brain.

After the game begins, either player can start throwing out answers. "I think it begins with the letter J," or "It has two syllables and ends with a Y."

Once part of the forgotten name/title/whatever in question has been determined, you get to move onto the next part.

The game ends when the entire answer has been correctly ascertained or you agree to let it go because you know it will pop into your mind hours later or perhaps when you're trying to sleep (and can't) that night.

This is what counts for fun when you're over a certain age. And if you're not over a certain age, it's more entertaining than you think. It's sort of like Sudoku for older people—a way to exercise your brain, problem solve with a spouse, significant other or friend, as well as pass the time.

And when you come up with the correct answer, the satisfaction you feel is immeasurable. But only until the next time one of you wants to play Tag Team Recall and asks, "What was the name of..."

COLONOSCOPY

I was at the grocery store today buying food for my upcoming colonoscopy prep. Thank you to the various people who assisted me in choosing gelatin flavors—I wasn't sure if orange was an acceptable color (it's not).

Anyway, I started thinking that after the colonoscopy I need to schedule my mammogram. And a bone density scan, which I've never had. I'm also way overdue for an eye exam and a little overdue for a physical. After that, it's the dentist. I was at my gynecologist not too long ago and the dermatologist as well, so I'm good there. But I will have to circle back to those soon enough.

I'm sure there are entire body parts I'm forgetting about. I haven't even mentioned the times I've needed months of physical therapy for my back or shoulder after an unfortunate run in with my sports bra (the sports bra won; see my previous book).

Ackkkkkkkk.

Is this why people retire—because they need more time to visit doctors?

I miss the days when I could just get a physical every five years. I was never a big dentist goer because, not to brag, I have really good teeth and rarely have cavities or tartar build up (it's my one claim to fame—please just let me have it).

I know individuals who for some reason like visiting doctors. They consider it an activity, like pickleball or canasta. That's not me. I try to walk that fine line between being vigilant about my health but not too nervous or obsessive.

Some people schedule all their doctor visits in the same few weeks, or month. I prefer to stagger mine so as not to get overwhelmed or completely ruin one month. Although if I were going to ruin a month, January would be it. It's pretty dreary anyway. But when you do it my way it seems that there's always an appointment on the horizon. Or a follow up to the initial appointment. After a certain age, follow-up appointments come with the territory.

I'm not sure which doctor schedule is the better way to go. I guess it's personal preference.

In any event, I'm just grateful I'm still around to schedule those appointments.

HYGGE IS STILL MY FAVORITE WORD

Not too long ago I was helping a young woman with her college essays. One essay prompt asked what the applicant's favorite word was and why.

Anyone who's been in Aisle 4 for a while knows what my answer would be. And for those who don't, it's hygge – the Danish word for everything cozy. I've been obsessed with this concept since I read about it several years back.

I did one of those DNA kits, which estimated my ethnicity to be 98% Jewish Peoples of Europe AND, wait for it, one percent Danish. Which explains a lot.

Getting back to hygge. Our winters here in the Northeast may not be as long or as harsh as the winters in Scandinavia; however, they are no walk in the park either.

Hygge is a way to make it a little more pleasant. Slippers, roaring fireplaces, hot chocolate (with marsh-mallows, of course), soft throw blankets, sweaters, scented candles; I could go on and on, but I think you are getting the hygge picture.

The Danish people prefer small groups to large parties (me), wearing comfy things like sweatpants (also me), and curling up with books, magazines, or to watch a movie (me, me, me!).

Tonight the temperatures will dip into the 30's for the first time this season. Not exactly prime hygge weather but certainly getting closer. Although I'm no longer a fan of snow, it certainly sets the stage for all things hygge.

I admit that I prefer warmer (but not too hot) temps and longer days. I mean, who wants to watch the sunset while eating lunch (which is how it will feel when we turn the clocks back in a few weeks)? I also like wearing t-shirts and sandals and going out for ice cream. Or staying in for ice cream. And I love love love the beach. The sand between my toes, the sun warming my body.

But in the absence of summer, hygge is a way to make the best of the fall and winter. It's a way to be happy all year round.

I will ask you all to remind me of this when we have our fifth snowstorm (the first few are always magical and then, not so much). When I'm griping about the ice and frozen tundra and lack of sunlight you can say, "But think how hygge it is!!!" And I may or may block you, depending on how cold I am.

However, for the moment, I'm deliriously excited for hygge season to begin. Hot chocolate is on today's shopping list. And if chestnuts happen to be at the grocery store I will definitely get some.

TATTOO

I noticed a tattoo on a guy's arm. I couldn't figure out what it said, so I asked him.

He said his tattoo was the word grateful with part of each letter missing. So that he would remember to be grateful even when there were things missing. He was a Grateful Dead fan and this was from one of their album covers.

I thought that was incredibly meaningful. I'm not a tattoo type of person but I would love to have that tattoo on a t-shirt. Or maybe a piece of jewelry. The older I get, the more I realize that it's not about what's not there. It's about feeling grateful for what is. Perfect.

THE SECRET TO THRIVING IN OLD AGE

Okay, mates, today I'm going to share the secret for thriving into old age. Yes, I realize this is a big topic for a Sunday morning when my coffee hasn't even kicked in yet. So please bear with me while I tell a longish story that I promise has a point.

My in-laws were very involved in their synagogue on Long Island. At one point, my father-in-law was president and at another head of the ritual committee. They had a ton of temple friends and attended services regularly where they had seats near the front of the sanctuary with their names on them. When my father-in-law passed away, my mother-in-law raised money to buy an eternal light for the bimah (raised platform in the synagogue from where the service is led) in his memory. Even after she moved to a different town thirty minutes away, she continued to attend services at their temple.

About five or six years ago, she moved to Westchester to be closer to the family. And her old temple is kind of going kaput. Membership has declined to the point where they will be closing; perhaps the few remaining members will continue worshiping together in a much smaller space.

So, my MIL joined the synagogue we attend. The one where we have been members for 25 years and all my boys were bar-mitzvahed. And she started attending services so regularly that everyone knows her name, like in *Cheers*. She knows the Rabbi and the Cantor and many of the congregants and they know her. It's possible she knows more people there than I do. When she didn't show up for services on Yom Kippur, my son and husband were so concerned that there had been a carbon monoxide incident at my brother-in-law's house where she was staying that they went by to check on them after temple was over. (Everything was fine; because of the torrential rains they decided to stream instead of attending in person.) And yes, we are all worriers.

My MIL could bemoan the fate of her old shul. She could talk about the old days incessantly. But at 90.5 years old she forges ahead, finding new things in which to engage. Although she visits the past, she doesn't live there. And therein lies the secret of her success. She's way busier than we are. She plays canasta and mahjong and does a million other things. I guarantee you that if you call her up right now and invite her over, she will come. Unless she has other plans, which is entirely possible.

Now, one could argue the chicken and egg thing here. Does her reasonably good physical health enable her to keep going or does she keep going thereby helping her physical health? Hmmm. Maybe a bit of both. But I suspect nothing would stop her short of the end which I hope is a very long time from now.

I know that my nature is different than hers. But if I make it to her age, I intend to emulate her secret to success as best I can.

I give this woman major props. It's not easy to lose a spouse (and later a partner) and start over. But she has.

Quite successfully in fact.

There are always things you can look forward to. You just have to keep looking.

'till 120...

Its not that being a grandparent is better than being a parent; It's just that it's less stressful, less taxing, and more fun. Oh wait– maybe it IS better.

~Thoughts From Aisle 4

PART 5: GRANDPARENTHOOD: THE EXCITEMENT IS REAL!

BABY ON THE WAY!!!!

*I*n case any of you were worried that I'd have nothing to write about after my house is finished, fear not. Once again, my kids have provided me with new material. (They are considerate like that.)

Drum roll...

My oldest son and daughter-in-law are expecting!! (An actual baby this time, not another granddog.)

I have to admit that when I first found out about my grandfetus, I got a little teary. In fact, I was so emotional I lifted the curse I had placed on my son sometime during his teenage years when I told him I hoped he (someday) had a kid just like himself. I actually do hope he has a child like himself, but the current version, not the earlier version who drove me insane. He's a delight now but back then, not so much.

I'm learning how different things are these days with this entire pregnancy situation. Although gestation is still 40 weeks (give or take), a lot of things have changed. To start with, you get so much more information before the child is born. Based on blood tests and scans we already know the gender, what this child looks like, where they will go to college as well as their favorite foods, musical preferences, and political leanings.

Other things that have changed include parental leave (which I will discuss more in a future post), maternity clothes, strollers, etc. I'm pretty sure some of the fancy new strollers cost more than my first car.

One thing that has not changed is my worrying. Given my history, it's not surprising. I have worried about this grandfetus pretty much every day since March when my kids told me they were expecting. The night before my daughter-in-law went for a fetal echocardiogram, I barely slept.

I'm happy to report that so far, so good. Knock wood, poo poo poo. But I'm guessing I will continue to worry until this child is born. And grows up and gets married.

Back to the gender—It's a boy! When my kids told my mother-in-law she chuckled. She had two sons. And then was told not to fear because someday she'd have granddaughters. But—she had seven grandsons. So she was told that G-d willing, she'd live to have a great granddaughter. And now her first great-grandchild is another boy! (Another example of why you shouldn't give credence to random things well-intentioned people say.)

I want you to know that I will be writing about lots of other topics besides my grandfetus. I promise. Me, I won't be one of those grandmothers who talks about their grandkids all the time. Also me, let me show you ten thousand pictures.

But I did want to share this exciting news.

I love how pregnant women today wear form-fitting clothing; in my day a family of six could've hidden under my maternity dresses without anyone noticing

~Thoughts From Aisle 4

BABYMOONS

Have you ever noticed how the younger generation invents a concept and it then becomes a thing?

Case in point: "Babymoons."

For the uninitiated, babymoons are the vacations expectant parents take before the blessed event occurs. Not to be confused with all the other vacations they've taken.

I'm thinking there should be "Grandbabymoons." And I've decided I want to go to Paris for my grand-babymoon. Where I visit handbag stores and museums. What does that have to do with becoming a grandparent? Absolutely nothing but I feel like I missed out when I had my kids. By my calculations, I'm owed a lot of trips and I've got to start somewhere.

Let me know if you think we can get this idea to catch on. Because honestly, our generation deserves it.

MY CHILD WITH A CHILD OF HIS OWN

My youngest son is working from home today and when he was just in the kitchen, he commented that I no longer write about how rotten he and his brothers were when they were younger. Actually, he didn't use the word rotten—that was my take on it.

So, to make him happy I will tell you all a story about the time Mr. Aisle 4 and I took our middle son to college and left our youngest and oldest sons home. (They were 13 and almost 23 at the time.)

At some point during the weekend, I called oldest son and asked how it was going. Of course he said, "fine." I asked where his brother was and he said, "I dunno, maybe in the basement?." I requested that he check, which he did, only to report that my youngest didn't seem to be in the house.

So I called the youngest on his cell phone (luckily I had recently purchased one for him). He told me he was walking into town with a friend to get food because he hadn't eaten. Or something to that effect. I realize that he wasn't a baby but I was annoyed that oldest son hadn't offered him food. It was basically like leaving my youngest son alone for the weekend, except there was a semi-adult in the house. Probably in his bed on his computer or napping.

I've been thinking about this story a fair amount since finding out that my oldest son will be a father soon. I mean this happened almost a decade ago and he seems a lot more responsible these days. He has a wife and a job and a house and even a dog. The last time he came to visit with his dog he even remembered to bring dog food, which is a good sign. And I have to say, he's now a remarkable older brother.

It's going to be interesting (and probably a lot of fun) to see my child with a child of his own. It's one of the things I'm looking forward to most. I actually think that he and his wife will be fabulous parents. And if he does forget to feed my grandson, I know that my daughter-in-law will remind him.

NEONATAL LOSS—THE HEARTBREAKING GIFT THAT KEEPS ON GIVING...AND SOME AMAZING NEWS

I've written about my first baby numerous times. The one who died in infancy of a heart defect.

I've also written about how his brief life and death changed me in so many ways. How I viewed pregnancy and delivery. When all goes right, and the result is a healthy baby and mom, it is truly is nothing short of a miracle. Full stop.

I was a wreck during my subsequent pregnancies. At my 20-week fetal echocardiograms I held my breath until I heard that all was fine. If my kids are neurotic, they come by it honestly.

A friend who had a stillbirth in her last trimester once said to me that, for us, pregnancy had been ruined forever.

What I didn't anticipate was that my anxiety would carry on to the next generation. Neonatal loss – the gift that keeps on giving.

I started worrying the minute I found out my daughter-in-law and son were expecting. I held my breath through all her appointments and the fetal echocardiogram, waiting impatiently for their texts letting me know everything was fine. I had pregnancy dreams. And dreams about being in the delivery room. You don't have to be Freud to figure out where those were coming from.

I tried not to let my kids see my anxiety. Who was I kidding? There's no way I could hide it. It oozed out of my pores.

Per the Jewish tradition, my daughter-in-law had no baby shower. I haven't purchased a single thing. (Not that it stopped me from looking at cute baby clothes online.) The gender reveal was a nonevent at twelve weeks: "Hey mom, it's a boy." No canons with glitter or cake with blue frosting on the inside. Not our way. About those reveals—although sometimes they look fun, I hate when I see one where the mom or dad looks disappointed. For ever and ever, that child will have video proof that perhaps their gender was not the preferred one.

When I put my hand on my daughter-in-law's stomach and felt the baby move, I was once again thunderstruck by the wonder of it all. And I whispered to him, "Please be okay."

And now I am thrilled to share the good news: My grandson arrived at 1:53 a.m. on Thanksgiving morning, weighing in at 7 lbs. 1 oz. All is well with mom and baby and I couldn't be more excited, relieved, and yes, thankful.

Let the shopping commence.

CHOOSING GRANDPARENT NAMES

Following their announcement that they were expecting a baby, my kids told me and my husband that we should start thinking about our grandparent names.

Wait, WHAT????? We get to CHOOSE what we are going to be called? This was news to me.

I wasn't actually sure how people came to be grammy or bubbe. In my family, my older brother did the choosing. In an earlier chapter I mentioned that when my father's mother moved to Queens from Canada she became the New Grandma because my brother didn't know her that well. My mother's parents lived with us and they were Nanny/Nana and Grandpa.

My husband immediately came up with his grandparent name which I still don't completely understand: Sababa. Saba is the Hebrew word for grandfather so I get that. Sababa means "great" or "cool." Is he saying he wants to be a cool grandfather? He told us that he knows someone who is called Sababa and he just liked the sound of it.

It took me a little longer to decide what my name would be. I felt like this was a very serious assignment and I wanted to give it all the gravitas it deserved. My daughter-in-law's mom already has two granddaughters and they call her Granny Annie. Cute, right?

I loved both of my grandmothers very much. They influenced my life in countless ways.

So one night as I tried to fall asleep (which is a constant battle for me) it came to me: Nana. I want to be called Nana. In memory of my own Nana. If I am half as good a grandmother as she was, I will be great.

Being a grandparent is a hugely important job. I learned that from my own grandparents. They teach, nurture, and give to you when your own parents are depleted.

Having said all this, if my grandson comes up with a different name for me, so be it. I will answer to anything. And be extremely grateful for the privilege of being a grandmother.

BABY NAMES—DO NOT SHARE

I won't know my new grandson's name until his bris (circumcision ceremony). Which got me thinking about baby names.

One piece of advice I would give to expectant parents is not to discuss potential baby names in advance of the birth.

Because—EVERYONE IS GOING TO HAVE AN OPINION!!! And not surprisingly, some people will not like the names you are considering. And they will not be shy in letting you know. They might make a face or even gasp in horror.

Names are a very personal choice, like ice cream flavors. Some people prefer traditional names or biblical names (I tend to drift in that direction). Some are drawn to trendy names – when I was pregnant Brittany, Chelsea, and Tiffany were popular for girls. Just so you all know if I had had a daughter she might have been Rachel, Abigail, or perhaps Emma.

Jews often name for people who have died. Which means there will be relatives lobbying hard for their favorite dead person. My mother-in-law did this on behalf of my father-in-law who had passed away a few years before my middle son was born. (May his memory be for a blessing.) She also was not shy in telling me that one of the names we were considering was a popular dog's name. Ouch. We ended up not going in that direction. (I was probably worried his first word would be "woof.")

Once the baby is born and their name is a done deal, people are less likely to tell you they hate your choice. At least to your face—I guarantee they will still talk about the name behind your back. But that's okay because in due time they will move on to the next baby's name they dislike. And who knows, perhaps they will even like the name you chose. It's certainly a possibility.

In any event, it's important to not feel pressure (which I think today's generation is better at than mine was) and to do whatever feels right for you and your child. Just try not to choose a name which might embarrass them later. Oh, and make sure their initials don't spell something odd. Or crude. Like Alex Steven Smith. Just no.

Choose wisely. But don't worry too much because if your kid absolutely hates their name they can always change it later. Or at the very least, they can add it to their list of grievances against you.

BRIS

I've been trying to figure out if I should focus on one aspect of my grandson's bris (Jewish circumcision ceremony) which was yesterday. However, I decided instead to offer little snippets (pun intended), like a highlights reel.

The bris was held in an old shul (temple) in Brooklyn not far from where my kids live. The morning started with davening (praying) before moving onto the circumcision, which took about ten seconds. This is the full-time job of the mohel (person who does the circumcision), and he is quite good at what he does.

Next came the naming. In keeping with my Aisle 4 style of not using my family's actual names, I will continue to call my grandson Turkey Baby. Or just "my grandson." But I will say that his name is beautiful. His middle name is my father's—I know my dad would be so incredibly happy and proud about that. And Dad certainly would have enjoyed the lavish breakfast that came after.

The ceremony brought home for me how our Jewish traditions have been maintained for centuries. We could have been in any shul anywhere in the world at any point in time and the rituals would have looked the same. A continuous thread that has not been broken.

It was an incredible thing to see my grandson surrounded by so much love and joy.

A few more thoughts...

My mechutan (father of my daughter-in-law) mentioned how this baby connects us. Which is true—as long as we live, we will be among his biggest cheerleaders and part of a select group who knows how brilliant, kind, and beautiful he is.

I brought red ribbon to tie around the baby's bassinet. To ward off the evil eye, something my Nana taught me was super important. After my middle son moved into the city he asked me to bring red ribbon to tie on his bed like he had at home in the hope it would help him sleep better. Not sure if it helped, but it certainly didn't hurt.

Later in the day, my brother's older son was holding the baby. And at that moment, he looked so much like his father (who died in 2008) that it made my husband cry. We felt the presence of so many generations and people who have passed on. I have no doubt that they were with us.

Many people have expressed to me how this new life has given them hope. At a time when things seem so bleak, he offers the promise of a better tomorrow.

Watching my son with his own son is a remarkable thing. It makes me smile to see him so completely in love and ready, willing, and able to meet this tiny person's every need. It's a daunting task and I am amazed at how well he and my daughter-in-law are adapting.

I could go on except I have to start getting ready for Shabbat. I hope you all have a wonderful weekend and Shabbat shalom. Peace, my friends.

BLANKIE

This story is 32 years in the making.

When my oldest son was born, a good friend gave him a baby blanket. Which became Blankie. As in the most treasured possession my son owned.

When Blankie was dirty, my son waited impatiently for its "bath" to be finished. When Blankie got a little tattered, my son brought him to me for repairs. When we went on vacation, Blankie came with us. But we will get back to that shortly.

When my other sons were born, the same friend purchased the same blanket for them as well. My middle son had little interest in that pastel blanket; he preferred a powder blue blankie with a sateen border. My youngest son however, loved his Blankie with the same fervor as his oldest brother. I actually purchased a second blankie for him as a spare, just in case. I will explain why.

When my older sons were about seven and two we took a trip to the Bahamas; my husband was between jobs and we used the opportunity to get away for a few days. Of course my older son's blankie was with us.

It was a lovely trip, until calamity struck.

Somehow Blankie got taken away with the bedding when the housekeeper cleaned our room. When we realized what had happened, we called housekeeping and then the hotel's manager to see if he could help. They said they searched the laundry, but Blankie was never to be seen again.

My son was heartbroken. When we got home, we gave him his younger brother's unloved blankie. Although it was not yet broken in, my son accepted new Blankie into his heart.

New Blankie went with my son to camp. And then college. When my son graduated and returned home there were only two items (other than his clothes) which returned with him: the Tempur-Pedic pillow we had purchased at Bed, Bath & Beyond (may its memory be for a blessing) and Blankie.

Blankie now lives with my son and daughter-in-law in Brooklyn. Faded and frayed, but still loved.

When my grandson was born three weeks ago, the same friend ordered the pastel blanket for him. It has a slightly different pattern and is personalized, but there's no doubt that it's Blankie, the next generation.

My son will be able to tell his own son about the adventures he and Blankie had together.

It remains to be seen whether this blanket becomes as beloved as the original ones were. Perhaps it will, perhaps it won't. Only time will tell.

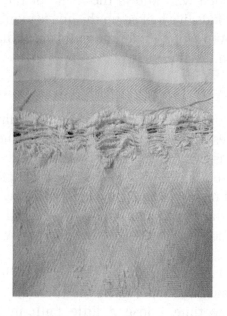

New Blankie and Well-Loved Blankie

PORCH PIRATE

The other day I wrote about how a porch pirate stole packages from in front of my son and daughter-in-law's house in Brooklyn. Packages which contained gifts for my infant grandson. Awful, right?

However, because life doesn't give a yin without a yang...

Someone who knows the name of the street on which my kids live looked up the house number on the internet. And sent a gift for my grandson to that address with my son's name on it.

But...it wasn't my son's house.

Someone with his exact name, including middle initial, lives three blocks away from him. They are the same age as well. How weird is that??

My son is not on Facebook (probably so that he can't read my posts) but my daughter-in-law is. So the guy with the same name as my son tracked her down through Facebook. Last night my son went over there to pick up the gift.

I told my son he should be friends with his name twin. Because he sounds like a good person.

Every time I lose a little faith in humanity something happens to restore that faith.

This is why I prefer to write about real stories over fiction. Because honestly I couldn't make up anything this good.

A LITTLE PRAISE GOES A LONG WAY

The other day I told my daughter-in-law that I think she is doing an amazing job as a mom.

First of all, she really is pretty incredible. She has completely and totally thrown herself into motherhood, selflessly meeting my three-month-old grandson's every need with nary a complaint.

I plan on praising her often because I think it's important for moms to hear positive feedback. Yes, my grandson gives feedback by way of smiles and coos, but he can't say, "Mom, I think you're the best." And when he's a teen, it's likely he will use words other than "best."

When I was raising my sons, I don't remember getting a lot of praise. There were no paychecks, no rewards for making it through the day. Going above and beyond the call of duty was expected. My husband did occasionally tell me I was a good mom, and my kids always said something sweet in their Mother's Day cards (which is one of the reasons I love that day so much). But the other 364 days they had a lot more complaints than accolades.

As a society I don't think we offer enough support to moms. It's the hardest job in the entire world, physically and mentally. There's no project end date, no formal reviews, no time off.

The least we can do is let moms know how awesome they are. Wherever and whenever. It may not make the job any easier, but I guarantee it will be appreciated.

BEING A GRANDPARENT—I'VE GOT THIS

Before my grandson was born, I had some concerns about my role as a grandparent.

Yes, I realize I raised three sons, but grandparent-hood is totally different than being a parent. I mean I'm a lot older now. What if I wasn't able to rise to the occasion? I can barely rise off the floor. Also, I had a tough act to follow with my own grandmothers, who as I said earlier, were amazing.

I'm quickly discovering that being a grandparent is nothing like being a parent. NOTHING.

My kids created a What's App group for the grandparents where they share pictures and updates about our grandson with us. So basically we ooh and ahh a lot and discuss how beautiful and brilliant our baby boy is. Mind you, he's only thirteen days old but we can already tell that he's got all of our best qualities. Not to brag, but he discovered his thumb at a mere nine days of age. And he seemed to be staring at a black and white toy with laser focus. I would say he's destined for Harvard but with their recent track record of poorly handling antisemitism on campus, I wouldn't want him to go there. He can definitely do better.

I'm getting the sense that unconditional love is basically all that's required of me. I can do that.

Also, since I didn't buy anything before my grandson was born, I'm making up for lost time. I've done so much online shopping that I can't even remember what I ordered. It's not inconceivable that a pony shows up on their doorstep. I hope not though because their Brooklyn backyard is kind of small.

I'm not gonna lie; I can't imagine raising a child from scratch again. That's a job best left to the younger generation. But this walk-on role seems pretty cushy. All of the fun, none of the spit up. Okay, maybe a little bit of the spit up.

Yeah, I think I'm gonna be okay at this job after all.

CRIB IN THE HOUSE!!

We just had a crib delivered to our house.

It's been many years since we had a crib in our home. When our youngest moved onto a regular bed, we happily gave away our crib to a friend who had given birth to twins. We requested that she never return it.

After three kids I figured that crib owed me nothing. I also figured I didn't need to store it until potential grandkids arrived on the scene. Judging by the way my sons behaved back then, I wasn't actually sure they'd ever find mates or procreate. But lo and behold, they grew up, learned to (mostly) behave, found wonderful young women, and as you know, on Thanksgiving the oldest made me a grandma.

I was surprised to discover that cribs are different these days. Starting with the fact that the sides do not go up or down. Crazy, right? You have to lean over the rail to scoop up the baby. I assume there were safety issues with movable sides, but it did make things easier. For the record, my kids were never able to maneuver the sides, but they did learn to hurtle themselves over the rail when they were over being confined. I will never forget the first time my oldest son escaped his crib. He appeared in the kitchen where I was cleaning and shouted "hi"—I nearly had a heart attack.

Sometime between my oldest son (who is now 32) and the youngest (22) crib bumpers also became a safety hazard. As did blankets, which were replaced by something called sleep sacks. Sleep positions changed from stomach to side to the current recommendation, which is that babies should be put down on their backs. I wonder if that's the last of the position changes or if they will come up with something new that we cannot even imagine.

Some things that have NOT changed are how cute babies are. And how needy. And how their piercing cries can wake the dead—but often not their fathers.

The crib I had for my sons was white. This new crib is a beautiful natural wood. And it looks so perfect in my son and daughter-in-law's room in my house. When I look at it I imagine my grandson, as well as future grandchildren, sleeping in it.

It felt good when we gave away a crib. It feels even better to have one in the house once again.

MY GRANDSON'S FIRST SLEEPOVER

This past weekend my three-month-old grandson came to visit. He brought his parents with him, which was helpful. Although he had been to our house before, this was his first sleepover.

It's been decades since I've had a baby in the house. And although I've never experienced Christmas because I'm Jewish, waking up and knowing he was here is how I imagine Christmas morning feels.

My first thought when my eyes opened was that I could go hold my Turkey Baby. And hold him I did. I didn't mind the spit up or his occasional fussiness, I just wanted the cuddles. And each coo and smile I got felt like winning the lottery. When I held him, it seemed like no time at all had passed since my own kids were babies, but it also felt like a lifetime ago, if that makes any sense.

I always assumed that the grandparent thing was a little overrated. Like when everyone raves about a movie or book you end up thinking it was just okay and wonder why there was so much hype around it. I was happy for my friends who had grandkids before me, and loved hearing about the babies because babies are blessings and so friggin' cute. But I wondered if I would feel the same adoration that they did. Obviously I do.

My friends who do not yet have grandkids have been equally indulgent of my (oversharing) pictures in our group texts. For which I am greatly appreciative. It's not inconceivable that they have a side text going without me where they discuss how annoying I've been, but I've not been privy to it.

When I had my own kids I was so fixated on the nuts and bolts of parenting that I couldn't fully enjoy them. But now that I don't have to deal with the nuts and bolts, which is an aspect of having kids that cannot be underestimated, it's mostly just fun and games.

I don't say this to make anyone who doesn't have grandkids feel bad. Just as when I talk about my kids I don't want people without children to feel badly. Although my kids can be a mixed bag, I can already see that my grandson will be incapable of doing wrong.

By the way, my oldest son used to travel with pretty much only a toothbrush. When they arrived this time, he was basically a sherpa going back and forth to the car for all the baby stuff they had brought with them. So. Much. Stuff. His days of traveling light are definitely over—at least for now.

MEET THE METS

Watching my son grow into his role as a father has been an interesting process.

This was my child who scoffed anytime I intimated that parenting three sons was less than an easy task. I knew that the day would come when he would begin to understand my point of view a little better. Especially his whole "How hard can traveling with kids be?" mantra. Don't even get me started with that one. Each trip was its own little insane adventure.

But the best part about seeing my son with his own son has been watching him fall more and more in love with that little person.

Yesterday my son, daughter-in-law, and Turkey Baby, who are in Florida, went to a Mets spring training game. My husband and boys are all huge Mets fans. Which comes with a lot of angst. I've endured almost 37 years of that angst, and let me tell you, it ain't easy.

Back to spring training. A million years ago, my dad took me to a Yankees game in Florida and it was a blast. I think I still have the hat from that day with several players signatures on it. So I get it.

My kids sent us pictures of them enjoying the game —my grandson in a Mets onesie and a hat too big for him. Since he's only four months old, he probably didn't care much about the score, but he did seem to enjoy playing with his toes. (The Mets lost so it was probably a good thing he was more focused on those toes.)

Despite the loss, my son had an amazing time. He told us what an emotional experience it was – bringing his son to his first ballgame.

Sharing the things you love with your kids is one of the best things about parenting. And it doesn't really matter what it is; a ballgame, favorite song, or tv show —whatever. It's being together and revealing yourself to someone you love so much, even if they are too young to understand.

Then hopefully someday, your little person will grow up and send you a picture of them doing their favorite thing with their little person.

And you will understand exactly how they feel.

Turkey Baby averting his eyes from a Mets loss

Dear Kids - I can pretty
much guarantee you will
become more like me and
your dad as you get older.
Have a nice day.
Love, Mom

~Thoughts From Aisle 4

I'm at the "Oh look,
there's a bathroom -
I probably should stop
in and pee" stage of life

~Thoughts From Aisle 4

PART 6: LAUGHTER, PURE AND SIMPLE

UNIVERSITY FOOD COMPLAINT

*B*reaking News: Massachusetts University Adds Michelin Restaurant to Dining Options

In response to complaints about the food, one university has decided to add a Michelin star restaurant to its campus.

A spokesperson for the university, which is located in Waltham, Massachusetts, said that they decided to let some of its top faculty go in order to provide the highest level of food for their students.

The chef who will be running the restaurant was trained in Paris and has worked at some of the finest culinary establishments throughout Europe and the United States. He said he feels confident that he will be able to get at least one Michelin star, if not two within the first year.

Although the university had previously prided itself on its Nobel-prize-winning professors and small class sizes, they said they now realize that education is secondary to food. According to one person in the administration who did not wish to be named, "By upping our food game, we feel confident we will attract more applicants, rise in the *U.S. News and World Report* rankings, and most of all, hear less kvetching. We suspect other colleges will follow suit."

The new dining option will be part of the meal plan, with an additional surcharge for students who wish to frequent the restaurant.

When asked how they felt about the news, one parent of a rising sophomore said that they "wouldn't be satisfied until the dorms were run by the Four Seasons chain and there was a spa where students could get weekly massages."

Further developments will be reported as they occur.

YOUR APPLICATION FOR ADMISSION INTO THE JEWISH SPACE LASER SOCIETY HAS BEEN REJECTED...AGAIN

See copyright page for image information

Dear Applicant:

Thank you for your continued interest in the Jewish Space Laser Society. We regret to inform you that we cannot offer you admission at this time.

As you know, the Jewish Space Laser Society requires that its members be sufficiently Jewish, as well as sufficiently aware of issues surrounding either "space" or "lasers." Your application, unfortunately, fails on both these counts.

According to our records, on April 14, 1998, you quietly snuck a bagel out of the breakroom at your place of employment, thereby violating the ban on eating bread during Passover. And while you tried to hide your "Hannukah bush" during the 2013 Christmas season, we know the truth. Finally, there is no such thing as keeping kosher "except for the occasional bacon, egg, and cheese."

While in other situations, we may be able to look past these transgressions—nobody's perfect—your decision to skip Yom Kippur services in 1999, 2011, and again in 2023 gives us pause. (You couldn't Zoom into the service? You slept in instead? It's a good thing your grandmother Rose isn't alive to know such things.)

As for the more technical requirements for admission into the Society, we found your application similarly lacking. Citing your background as a laser hair removal customer as "experience" is questionable at best. And while your essay about your interest in space correctly

notes that William Shatner and Leonard Nimoy
are/were examples for us to all admire, Harrison
Ford's inclusion is a serious mistake; he is, as Adam
Sandler made quite clear, only a quarter-Jewish. Not
too shabby but hardly enough to constitute a full
Space Jew. (I mean, Ford didn't even go to Brandeis!)

Sincerely yours,

The Jewish Space Laser Society
(a subsidiary of The People Who Control the Media)

P.S. You really should call your mother more often.

BREAKING NEWS: SPIRIT AIRLINES TO START CHARGING FOR SEAT BELTS

In an effort to increase profits, Spirit Airlines has made
the unprecedented decision to start charging passengers
for seatbelts. The company, which was already charging
$60 for carry-on luggage, realized that there were many
other ways it could increase revenue.

A spokesperson for Spirit, Jacob Marley, said that if
"customers do not want to pay the $25 seatbelt fee, they
are welcome to bring bungee cords to hold themselves
in place." A credit card mechanism will be added to each
seatbelt that will unlock them upon payment.

Additionally, Spirit announced that going forward,
there will also be a fee for using the bathrooms. One
passenger interviewed stated that she would wear
Depends on her flight rather than incur any more

expenses. And since the airline is already charging $5 for water, she said that "dehydrating might be a more cost effective option for me."

Marley also announced that, "in the unlikely event that the cabin lost pressure, there will be a $75 charge for oxygen masks," adding, "Although you can't put a price on safety, we are going to." For now at least, the airline will not charge for air in the cabin, although they warned that "nothing is completely off the table."

Other things being considered as extras are the seats, the engine, as well as a pilot. Passengers with enough virtual reality and video game experience would be welcome to have a go at flying the jets if they didn't want to incur another fee. However, at press time no final decisions had been made about those changes, which the airline admitted might be a little much for some customers and raise eyebrows at the FAA.

The President of Spirit, Ms. Penny Pincher, said, "Because our ticket prices are so incredibly low, we've had to come up with other ways to make our company profitable to keep the shareholders happy." She added, "We are not charging passengers for the bolts that keep our doors affixed to our planes, although we are thinking about testing duct tape as an alternative."

Further details will be reported as they happen.

I get confused when I hear someone say, "I forgot to eat today." I know what the individual words mean but I don't understand them grouped together like that

~Thoughts From Aisle 4

PART 7: RANDOM THOUGHTS

LET'S NOT PIGEONHOLE OUR MEALS

Yesterday I was in a store around 4:00 pm when I heard a sales associate say she was going to take her lunch. To which another sales associate said, "Isn't it too late to be eating lunch?" So I suggested maybe she was eating lupper or linner, a combination of lunch and supper/dinner. Unless of course she was planning on another meal sometime later in the evening in which case she was just having a late lunch.

Upon further reflection, I've decided we use too many labels when it comes to meals. For example, often at midday I'll eat a yogurt. And then later I'll have a slice of cheese or some peanut butter. (I'm kind of a grazer.) Would these be called snacks? Or lunch 1 and lunch 2? I really don't want to say I eat two lunches because it makes me sound like a glutton. (Which I kind of am but am okay with pretending I'm not.)

Why can't we just call it eating? Like, "Now I am eating."

During the early days of Covid, when we were only dining outside, my husband and I tended to eat our last full meal of the day earlier while it was warmer and still light. I really enjoyed that because later in the evening we would have lots of room for dessert. By the way, dessert should always be called dessert because it's sacred. Dessert can be eaten after a meal or instead of a meal or even before a meal. All that matters is it's something yummy that makes you happy. You can always just say, "I'm having dessert now," and no one should ever question you.

I feel like all the sales associate needed to say was "Now I am going to pause working and have some food because I am hungry, and my stomach is rumbling." No further classification necessary.

It may just be semantics; however, I feel better already.

According to a weight loss app I'd need to walk to Portugal to get skinny

~Thoughts From Aisle 4

HOT DOGS—NOT A HEALTH FOOD??

Last week I was watching TV, minding my own business, when I got an alert on my phone from CNN. My first thought was "What catastrophe has happened now?"

I looked away from watching an episode of *The Big Bang Theory* for the millionth time and steeled myself for yet another disaster. The important news? Each hot dog you eat takes 36 minutes off your life.

Seriously???? In a world that is completely falling apart they needed to send an alert about hot dogs? Like WTF.

First of all, 36 minutes is a really specific number. How can they possibly know this for sure? Did they take identical twins and stuff one with hot dogs for decades while feeding the other one only salads and fish? I bet the hot dog twin died happier.

My next thought was that Joey Chestnut is totally screwed. For those of you who don't know who Joey Chestnut is, he's the reigning Nathan's Famous hot dog eating champ. A few years ago he downed 76 hot dogs in ten minutes—2,736 minutes off his life in one sitting.

I happen to really like hot dogs. With a little sauerkraut and mustard on a bun it's the perfect meal. We don't eat them a lot, but I probably do have a few each month. The kosher, reduced fat, no nitrates kind, but I'm still guessing it can't be classified as a health food.

At 36 minutes per dog, I've probably unknowingly taken months off my life. The math made me really depressed. Although I usually make a vegetable on the side, like broccoli. I wonder if eating broccoli lessens the death decree – like maybe it only takes 22.8 minutes off your life.

I feel like this was sensationalist journalism. And certainly not alert worthy. They need to save their alerts for hurricanes and celebrity deaths. Not hot dogs.

Am I going to stop eating hot dogs? I'm honestly not sure. But if I do eat them I might enjoy them less. All because of that stupid news story, which I'm not even sure I believe.

By the way, my grandmother ate whatever she wanted to and lived to 100. Would she have lived until 120 if she had a healthier diet?

I'm mad at myself for letting them get inside my head. At this point I have so little fun and so few pleasures that if I want a hot dog, I should be able to eat one guilt free. I don't want to think about death while eating. I'm funny that way.

I think I'm going to turn off alerts on my phone.

In every relationship there's the person who falls asleep instantly and the other person who lies awake wondering how that's even possible

~Thoughts From Aisle 4

When I buy something special I tell my husband it's a gift for my next birthday. I just bought a handbag for turning 103.

~Thoughts From Aisle 4

HOW I MET MY HUSBAND

I'm often asked how I met my husband, the sidekick in many of my stories. So—here goes.

It was August 23, 1981, and I was moving into my college dorm. I was wearing a red UPenn t-shirt. I don't remember what he was wearing but I do remember thinking he was cute. He was helping freshman schlep in their stuff when we first spoke.

The future Mr. Aisle 4 asked me, "Who goes to Penn?" I said, "My brother just graduated" and he said, "MY brother just graduated too! As did his girlfriend." That was the beginning. Maybe it was a pickup line. I don't know. If it was, it worked.

He was the Resident Advisor on the second floor and was two years older. He eventually asked me out and our first date was the Don McLean concert on campus on October 17. And the rest was history. Lol no.

We went to the concert—"So bye, bye Miss American Pie, drove my Chevy to the levee but the levee was dry..." and then we hung out after in his dorm room and talked. It was nice.

However, I wasn't sure I was looking for nice. He seemed like excellent friend material, but was that enough? I felt like it was worth going on at least a few more dates so I could figure things out.

Things must've been moving too slowly because he complained to a good friend of mine that I didn't want to kiss him. It was true—but only because I still didn't think of him as boyfriend material. Friends don't kiss. (I wasn't a friends-with-benefits kind of gal.)

Even though he had NO money, he bought me carnations every Friday. Three for a dollar at the Student Center.

He walked me home from my job across campus at the theater box office at night across campus, so I'd be safe.

He checked on me if I didn't feel well.

Wait a minute!! Turns out nice WAS what exactly I was looking for. And while he was being nice I noticed there was a lot more to him. He was smart, funny, traditional, and we seemed to want the same things in life.

He chose a graduate school in Boston so we could be near each other while I finished college. We got engaged 4.5 years after we started dating and were married 18 months after that.

By the way, all these years later, he's still nice. He is quiet in the morning so I can sleep. He helps clean. He encourages me. He was by my side when I experienced a long period of depression.. Oh, and he laughs at my jokes.

He's everything.

Yeah, we fight. Of course we do. My youngest son sometimes rolls his eyes when we bicker. But we argue less than we used to when we were raising our kids and had more energy for fighting.

Since we lived in the same dorm at the same small university, I'm sure we would have met at some point. But I'm really glad I was wearing that red Penn t-shirt. I know that sometimes nice doesn't always last and that people change. But nice is a really good starting point.

TRAVEL

There are people who love to travel and people who don't.

I am in the people who don't category. I have done some traveling. London, Amsterdam, Hungary, all around the United States, Caribbean islands, etc. And after I get home, I'm always glad I went.

It's not that I don't like to discover new cities and landscapes, and learn about different places and cultures. I do. But I find traveling difficult. I get anxious, and my body doesn't like adjusting to different time zones. No matter where I am in the world, it prefers to stay on Eastern Time.

So when I stumbled upon *The Reluctant Traveler*, an eight-part Apple TV series starring Eugene Levy, I recognized a kindred spirit.

Each episode has Levy headed to a different destination where he stays in crazy fancy hotels and explores the local culture. I liked the fancy hotels part. As does he. And I also liked getting to sightsee—from the comfort of my bed.

It was the perfect series to watch while I was sick with the stomach flu from hell. I got to experience cool stuff while near my bathroom. Yes, I realize watching something on TV is not the same as experiencing it in person. But there's simply no way I'm ever going on a safari. Ever. Before you comment how you would love to go, or that you've been and it's amazing, I know. It's just not for me. I would be the person you hear about on the news who got eaten by a lion. Or contracts some weird disease.

I give Levy a ton of credit—he does things that are well out of his comfort zone. Like going on a helicopter ride. Even though he keeps his eyes closed for part of it and looks genuinely scared, he does it. He might be my new hero in fact.

I've always said that before you leave your house, you need to pray to the vacation gods because you never know what will happen. I've had vacations that went amazingly well and some that were veritable disasters. I will say that traveling without kids is definitely easier. Mine were a particularly difficult bunch. Except when we went to Disney World—they all loved Disney.

Someone I know was in New Zealand last month. On her way there, she sprained her ankle in the airport. And then there was a typhoon in New Zealand and her hotel was without power for four days. She said she thought she might die. And then on the way back to New York she fell asleep and woke up—in New Zealand. There had been a fire at JFK so halfway back to the U.S., the pilot turned the plane around. She described the trip as "an adventure." There isn't enough anti-anxiety medicine for me to have that kind of adventure.

Although after watching Levy explore the world, I might have a few more trips in me.

Until I get a chance to book my next trip, there's a new season of *The Reluctant Traveler* I can't wait to watch.

LOOK AT ME, WRITING ABOUT SPORTS

When I met my husband 42 years ago, he enjoyed watching soccer. Then we had three sons, and he passed his love of soccer onto them. They played it, watched it, reffed it, talked about it, etc.

Somehow this was all lost on me. When we were in London many years ago, and they all went to tour

Emirates Stadium, I toured Harrods. And when they went to watch a soccer match, I had afternoon tea all by myself. I love those tiny little sandwiches. But I digress.

I mean, I don't hate soccer. As far as sports go, it's fine. It moves along quickly and isn't overly violent like American football. Except for that offside rule, it's a pretty easy sport to understand.

Recently, in a moment of benevolence, I suggested we watch *Welcome to Wrexham*, a documentary about a soccer team in Wales (the third oldest soccer team in existence) that actors Ryan Reynolds and Rob McElhenney purchased because I don't really know why.

I figured my husband would enjoy it. Plus, who doesn't like Ryan Reynolds?

But lo and behold, it's become one of my favorite shows of all time. Really.

I'm a huge Ryan Reynolds fan. He and his wife Blake Lively and their family live one town over from me. Years ago, before they had kids, I was in a restaurant waiting for my takeout order when I turned around to see Ryan and Blake standing behind me. Canoodling. They were just so beautiful that I had to avert my eyes lest I be turned into a pillar of salt.

So we start watching *Welcome to Wrexham* and I'm barely paying attention. Because it's about football (I'm going to call it football instead of soccer from here on out).

Almost against my will, I found myself growing interested in the stories about the players. As well as the town of Wrexham and why football is so important to them.

The show is funny and touching and real.

It also confirmed my belief that Ryan is a mensch. He is Canadian after all. Rob is also a good guy (in case he reads this I don't want him to feel left out or anything).

I forgot to mention that the team is trying to get promoted into the English Football League after having been relegated to a lower league for 15 years. I know what happens because it aired this past spring plus I heard about it in real time, but of course I'm not going to tell you because I don't want to spoil it for you.

I'm not saying I'm going to sit on the couch with my husband and youngest son each week while they root for Arsenal. But *Welcome to Wrexham* did what I thought was impossible—I kind of sort of understand why people like football so much.

Kind of sort of.

LEAVE PHIL ALONE

Get this: PETA has called for Punxsutawney Phil (the official, original groundhog of Groundhog Day fame) to retire. I can't even.

PETA has suggested replacing Phil with a gold coin since his predictions are no more accurate than a coin toss. Honestly, the weather people I watch on the news every night don't get it right half the time either and they have degrees in meteorology. Today was supposed to be mild and sunny—as I type this a cold rain is falling. But I don't see anyone firing those guys. If they have job security why doesn't Phil?

No one REALLY thinks Phil can predict the weather. But it's FUN. It's TRADITION.

PETA's only complaint about Phil's treatment is that he isn't allowed to be free. Neither are a gazillion pets around the globe. From what I can see, that groundhog has it pretty good. Judging by his girth, he is well fed. All he has to do to earn his keep is smile for the cameras once a year and whisper something in the master of ceremonies' ear on February 2. That's it. If I could find a cushy job like that I'd take it in a nanosecond. And how do they know Phil doesn't love being a celebrity? Take away his job and he might get depressed. And who wants a depressed groundhog?

I think this is just a way for PETA to get some attention. Now that there are no more elephants in the circus and faux fur is in, things are probably a little slow for them. I am all for the ethical treatment of animals. However, leave Phil alone.

Here's hoping for an early spring.

Happy Groundhog Day 2024!

Phil and the Family

IT'S GROUNDHOG DAY!!!!

Happy Groundhog Day, everyone! I woke up to a ton of Groundhog Day wishes, which was super nice.

Big news: Punxsutawney Phil did NOT see his shadow, which means an early spring. Yayayay.

I had a feeling that's what he was going to say because, despite the recent gloom, I've been hearing birds tweeting every time I take my rescue pup Maisy on a walk.

Once that first long, dreary month of the year ended, I started feeling more positive. Like good things are coming. And apparently Phil has that same feeling.

By the way, I only listen to what Phil has to say. There are many weather-predicting groundhogs, but he's my guru. Plus, because he is given the Elixir of Life every fall, he lives forever.

Speaking of dead groundhogs, Milltown, New Jersey, has been without their weather-predicting groundhog Mel since he went to that great burrow in the sky a few years ago. And apparently, it's not so easy to get a new groundhog. (You can't just place an ad in LinkedIn.) According to New Jersey groundhog law, there's a limited list of out-of-state breeders permitted to import them. They can't just find one in the wild since groundhogs can bring with them a variant of rabies that isn't present in New Jersey. Who knew, right?

Back to that ad on LinkedIn. I was imagining what an ad for a replacement groundhog might say.

Groundhog Wanted: Only required to work one day a year for ten minutes. Meteorology degree not needed. No experience necessary. Excellent benefits and job security. Must not bite.

I mean, who wouldn't want that job? As for the Elixir of Life, I did a little research and apparently it only works for groundhogs and not humans. Bummer.

As a reminder, AMC is running the movie *Groundhog Day* all day and night today. I'm guessing you can find it on one of the streaming services as well. A friend of mine told me she had actually never seen the movie and I was like, "How can that even be?" It's worth watching—again and again.

So, as a recap: SPRING IS COMING!!!!!!! And, according to Phil, sooner rather than later. We've got this.

GROUNDHOG DAY POSTSCRIPT

Last night my youngest son sent me a picture of popcorn, sour patch kids, and the movie *Groundhog Day* on the tv in the background. I laughed but was also touched that he and his girlfriend had chosen to watch it.

In an interview I did for AccuWeather about Groundhog Day, I mentioned that when my kids were young and the movie ran in a continuous loop all day and into the evening, I made them watch it. No, I didn't bolt them to the couch, but I would say things like,

"Isn't this part funny?" or "Come sit with me for ten minutes during this scene." And I would try to discuss the themes of the movie with them. (Yes, I can see how having an English major for a mom could be annoying.) I also mentioned that they had probably tried reporting me to social services for doing this.

But despite their groaning about it, this tradition seems to have made at least a little impact on them.

I find this to be true about a lot of things we did when they were growing up. I've noticed that many of our customs have made their way into their homes. They all observe Shabbat, albeit in different ways, and the Jewish holidays. I admit that I sometimes wondered why I was putting so much effort into certain things when none of them seemed to care or even appreciate it.

But here's the thing about raising kids – the payoffs aren't revealed for a long time. And until then you spend a lot of time fairly certain they aren't even noticing your efforts.

But one day, far into the future, you might get a text with a shot of Bill Murray waking up (again) on Groundhog Day. And you'll realize that your attempts to share things that mattered to you now matter to them. And your heart will be happy.

VACATION UNPACKERS VS. SUITCASERS

When my husband and I go on vacation, the first thing he does when we get to our hotel room is unpack. Socks and underwear in drawers, pants and shirts hung neatly in the closet, etc. Every single item. He even puts his suitcase away. Whereas I open my suitcase, take out my toiletries and put them in the bathroom, and call it a day.

Yes, I'm one of those people who lives out of their suitcase when they aren't home.

You might think this means I'm a bit of a slob, but the fact is at home I'm overly tidy. Like a solid 7.5–8 on the 1–10 neatness scale. Basically I clean and do laundry ALL OF THE TIME. So when I'm away, which isn't terribly often, I'm not going to waste a single second of my precious vacation time on anything that even remotely resembles a chore. I become this whole other person when I'm away and it's liberating.

Of course, in a very short amount of time, my suitcase ends up a jumble of clothes and I can never find anything. So I will ask my husband to assist me in locating my missing shoe or t-shirt or whatever. Basically I start most sentences with, "Where is my..."

Now my husband would be well within his rights to say, "Find it yourself" or "You should've unpacked like I did."

But he never does. He always helps me locate the missing item. He might occasionally shake his head but he never says a word.

And this is one of the many reasons I love him.

It's a fact of life that couples have different ways of doing things. Loading the dishwasher, extruding toothpaste from the tube, and yes, vacation tidiness.

I don't pretend to have all the answers to finding and staying in love. But I do know that, whether you're the person who unpacks or the one who makes a jumble of their clothes, it's important to respect each other. And assist them in finding their underwear when it's hiding under two sweaters and a pair of sweatpants.

I HAVE NO CREDENTIALS

I've been thinking about credentials. Like the kind you need for a lot of professions. Lawyers, teachers, doctors, therapists, social workers, etc. all have certificates and degrees and licenses to do their jobs.

Since I am a blogger by trade, I wanted you to know what my blogging credentials are.

None. Zero.

Everyone who follows my page *Thoughts From Aisle 4* is following someone who has no credentials whatsoever to do what she is doing. This is an actual conversation which occurred in my house last night.

Youngest son: Do we have cell service?

Me: So funny you asked. My phone dropped several calls today.

Son: Not CELL SERVICE. SELTZER. Do we have plain seltzer?

Me: Ohhhhh. No. We just have the flavored.

Yup, that's me. Not only credentialless, but also somewhat daffy.

I HAVE been writing since I can remember. And I am a huge observer of everything. In fact, I am always mentally taking notes. I also think I have a pretty decent sense of humor. And I'm truthful. Lying is one of the things I hate most in the universe. If you want to make me crazy, lie to me and see what happens. (My kids can confirm this is true.)

But that's all I've got. There are 57K people who are following a person who is basically winging it.

Here is my blogging process. I wake up. Complain about not having slept well. Have my coffee. And scan my brain for something that it feels like writing about. Or something it feels needs to be said.

Sometimes I have a tiny thought that becomes a meme. And sometimes there are too many words for a meme, so I write a post.

The bottom line is basically anyone can do what I'm doing. You just sit in front of a computer, let your brain and fingers take over, and see what happens. Some days it's a lot of fun. Some days, not so much.

I'm guessing people with real credentials say that about their jobs too.

I just wanted you to have this information in case you'd prefer to find someone who has an actual degree in blogging. I'm pretty sure that's not a thing but maybe it should be.

Anyway, thank you all for reading the words of someone who pretty much has no idea what she is doing.

My level of being tired goes from exhausted to I might be dead and don't know it

~Thoughts From Aisle 4

As I have gotten older I
realize I care less about
what I eat for dinner and
more about not being the
one who has to make it

~Thoughts From Aisle 4

WE ALL DESERVE A STATUETTE

Anyone catch the Emmys last night? I thought it made for some decent entertainment on a cold, snowy night.

I liked how the host Anthony Anderson's mom was enlisted to shoo the winners off the stage when their acceptance speeches ran too long: "Okay, baby—wrap it up." There was a lot of nostalgia and reunions—I especially enjoyed seeing the casts of *Cheers* and *Ally McBeal* together again. I loved that Carol Burnett was there and I teared up during the memorial segment. As usual, I had forgotten that some of the people had died.

One of my favorite moments was one when Niecy Nash-Betts accepted her award and said, "You know who I want to thank? I want to thank me." Honest and true. While it takes a lot of support to be successful, in the end she did the work that got her that award.

I don't think most of us give ourselves enough credit. We get up each day and do what needs to be done. Taking care of family, going to a job, running a house, helping others, etc. We get it done, despite challenges—physical, emotional, whatever.

This life isn't always easy, but you are here, doing your best. And you deserve to be thanked by you.

I will go first.

I want to thank myself for showing up in Aisle 4 to entertain and enlighten all of you. And for doing my best despite being tired and anxious a lot of the time.

For always trying to tell the truth and make the world a little better.

And now, I want each and every one of you to thank yourself for doing a good job.

Give yourself a little grace. You've earned it.

THE END

So this is the end. But only the end of this book. Because in life there is really no end to all the stories one can tell.

And as long as I am able, I hope to continue sharing my stories with you.

xo Marlene

OTHER BOOKS BY MARLENE KERN FISCHER

Gained a Daughter But Nearly Lost My Mind: How I Planned a Backyard Wedding During a Pandemic

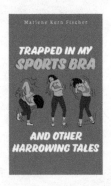

Trapped in My Sports Bra and Other Harrowing Tales

ABOUT THE AUTHOR

Marlene Kern Fischer is a wife, mom, grandmother, and blogger who lives in Westchester, New York.

Having escaped from her sports bra and completed physical therapy for her shoulder, which she chronicled in her second book *Trapped in My Sports Bra and Other Harrowing Tales*, Marlene decided she needed a new adventure. So she, her husband, and rescue pup Maisy, packed up their considerable belongings and moved to a new house. Which did not go as expected.

Moving, trying to purge her too many belongs, parenting adult children, becoming a grandmother for the first time, and entering a new decade of life, are among the themes Marlene explores in her newest book.

You can follow Marlene's blog, *Thoughts From Aisle 4*, on Facebook or find her on Instagram @aisle4 Marlene.

There's also a pretty good chance of running into her in aisle 4 at her local grocery store.

Made in the USA
Monee, IL
10 June 2024

59701313R00108